SAXON AND NORMAN CHURCHES IN ENGLAND

by the Rev.
E. Hermitage Day.

THIRTY TWO
ILLUSTRATIONS

SAXON AND NORMAN
CHURCHES IN ENGLAND

Norman Tower: Tewkesbury Abbey.

Saxon and Norman Churches in England

BY THE REV.

E. HERMITAGE DAY, D.D., F.S.A.

Author of " Gothic Architecture "

WITH THIRTY-TWO ILLUSTRATIONS

A. R. MOWBRAY & CO. Ltd.
LONDON: 28 Margaret Street, Oxford Circus, W. 1
OXFORD: 9 High Street
MILWAUKEE, U.S.A. : The Morehouse Publishing Co.

First impression, 1919

PREFACE

THE writing of this little book was finished on the eve of the outbreak of the war, which has delayed its publication. It is intended to complete the sketch of English Church architecture begun in two volumes, *Gothic Architecture* and *Renaissance Architecture*, which have already been issued in Messrs. Mowbrays' series "The Arts of the Church."

The proofs have had the great advantage of revision by my friend Mr. A. Hamilton Thompson, F.S.A., to whom I am indebted for many valuable suggestions incorporated in the text.

·E. H. D.

CONTENTS

CHAPTER I

CHAPTER II

CHAPTER III

LIST OF PLATES

Saxon and Norman Churches in England

❦ ❦ ❦

CHAPTER I

Romanesque

ROMANESQUE is a term of no very precise definition, which is employed to denote all those phases of Western European architecture derived mainly from Roman art, and developed with slowly increasing skill and mastery of principles from the fourth century to the beginning of the thirteenth. Romanesque architecture exhibits as its characteristic feature the round arch. The term is used in this book to cover the two styles which in England preceded the first pointed style, and to which the names of Saxon, or pre-Conquest, and Norman are applied. These styles were but the local versions of the style which prevailed all over Western

B

Europe, forms of the Romanesque derived mainly from the Continent, but showing the influence of the work, crude and immature though that work was, which had preceded them in Britain.

Into the question of the origin and early development of the Romanesque in general, much debated of late among antiquaries, it would be beyond the scope of this little book to enter. The great work of Rivoira attempts to show that the Italian Romanesque was derived directly from the Roman work, and that the strength of the Byzantine influence has hitherto been exaggerated. Rivoira's theory that the Lombard guilds, "the Comacine masters," sought eagerly among the ancient buildings of Rome and Ravenna for elements which they could combine into a new style for new needs, attributes to them a motive of which they were probably less conscious than he supposes. But, at least, he has shown that the Romanesque owes to the earlier Roman work a greater debt than had been recognized, and that the Byzantine influence may have been less strong than earlier writers thought, though Rivoira himself admits its powerful effect upon detail and ornament. His work on *Lombardic Architecture* is indispensable to the study of the whole subject of Romanesque, though it should not be read without reference to its corrective, Lasteyrie's *L'architecture religieuse en France à l'époque romane*. It must suffice here to take the Romanesque buildings of which the remains exist in England, to describe their general characteristics, and to assign them to their periods, so far as that can be done with any approximation to certainty.

WATTLE AND WOOD

Architecture as an art of the Church in England did not begin with the building of the first churches. The planters of the Faith built their churches as the people built their homes, of the simplest and least durable materials. Even if it be not authentic history, but only beautiful legend that—

"Joseph came of old to Glastonbury,
And there the heathen prince, Arviragus,
Gave him an isle of marsh whereon to build,
And there he built with wattles from the marsh
A little lonely church in days of yore,"

yet it is almost certain that an ancient church of wattlework stood once at Glastonbury, and that others were to be found elsewhere in Britain.

We may conjecture also that churches of untrimmed logs rose in the forest clearings, like that which may still be seen at Greenstead. But these wooden churches were in Britain only the necessity of primitive days. It is true that a few wooden churches remain to us from the Middle Ages : the Cheshire "stave-kirks" represent the use for Church purposes of the method locally employed for domestic buildings. But a systematic architecture in wood was never developed in Britain as it was in Scandinavia.

ROMANO-BRITISH CHRISTIANITY

Very little survives to recall the Christianity of the Romano-British period. The theory, in itself very probable, that Christianity came to Britain with the Roman legionaries derives little support from the researches of the antiquary. The excavation of the great military stations along the line of Hadrian's Wall has yielded up a large number of altars to the gods of Rome, and has brought to light at Borcovicus the remains of a Mithraic temple. But, in the excavations of the stations on the Wall, only one stone has been found which even suggests the presence of Christians in the Roman army of occupation.

In the neighbourhood of the Wall there is, indeed, much which witnesses to the ultimate triumph of the Faith over paganism. At Chollerton on the North Tyne, a mile or two above the bridge and military station

Plate 2.

Pillars from the Roman Forum of Cilurnum : Chollerton
(See page 4.)

of Cilurnum, the modern Chesters, there
is a Roman altar of which the top has been
hollowed out to convert it into a Christian
font ; and the south arcade of the church
is carried on monolith columns of Roman
hewing, doubtless taken from the forum
of Cilurnum. It has been suggested by
Professor Baldwin Brown that these
columns were in the seventh century taken
by S. Wilfrid for his church at Hexham,
and that at the rebuilding of Hexham they
were transferred to Chollerton. Hexham
Priory Church contains much Roman
material which S. Wilfrid brought from
Corstopitum, the modern Corbridge. At
Lanchester also, a few miles north-west of
Durham, Roman shafts have been used
in the arcade of the church. But this use
of Roman material, noticeable in tilework,
as at Brixworth, is no link with Romano-
British Christianity.

Of churches actually built during the
period only slight and uncertain traces
remain. The Venerable Bede says that
S. Augustine found at his coming into
Canterbury "on the east side of the city
a church dedicated in honour of S. Martin,
built whilst the Romans were still in the
island, wherein the queen used to pray";
and he adds that when the king was con-
verted to the Faith he allowed the priests

of S. Augustine's mission to build or repair churches in all places. The south wall of S. Martin's is constructed of Roman brick, and some antiquaries have therefore concluded that it is one of those churches which S. Augustine repaired, and that it retains some of the original Roman work. But this is disputed by no less an authority than Professor Haverfield, who is of opinion that at S. Martin's there is no Roman work *in situ*.

At Silchester, on the northern border of Hampshire, we are on surer ground. There, near the site of the forum of the little Roman city Calleva Atrebatum, one of those cities which perished almost out of memory, the foundations of a small church have been excavated, and its ground-plan recovered. It was of the basilican type, having more affinity with the North African type than with the Roman. Its nave terminated in a semi-circular apse ; aisles bounded by two sacristies flanking the sanctuary, and a small narthex, completed the plan. At the chord of the apse was found a square of mosaic, contrasting with the plain red tile with which the rest of the church had been paved. On this the altar had evidently stood. The apse faced west, following the primitive arrangement by

Plate 3.

Romano-British Church: Silchester.

(See page 7.)

which the priest ministered at the altar
looking eastward and facing the people,
having the other clergy behind him in the
bow of the apse, where seats of stone or
wood were provided for them. The date
of the church at Silchester lies probably
between the years A.D. 313 and 411.

Though few churches have been found,
it is probable that some Roman villas
owned by Christians had their chapels
or oratories, served either by a chaplain
who lived as one of the household, or by
missionary priests. If the number of
Christians increased the domestic oratory
would be replaced by a church; but perhaps this development rarely took place
in the country districts of Roman Britain.
In one or two Roman villas Christian
symbols have been found. At Frampton,
in Dorset, a mosaic pavement has been
uncovered, showing the *labarum* or Chi-
Rho monogram, in conjunction, it must be
admitted, with Neptune and Cupid. The
Chi-Rho has also been found scratched on
the masonry of a villa at Chedworth, in
Gloucestershire. But here again the evidence is of the very scantiest.

The Christianity, then, of Romano-
British times has left almost no architectural remains. And the reason is by no
means clear. One school of historians

C

maintains that Christianity was confined almost exclusively to the Roman settlements and the Romanized natives, affecting but slightly the general life of the country. This view gains support from the fact that the British sees were in well-known centres of Roman civilization—London, York, and Lincoln — and that there is a preponderance of Roman names in the early British records. But another school maintains the opinion that the real strength of Christianity at that time lay among the natives, whose poverty prevented them from building churches of stone, and they point to the failure of archaeology to find proof of vigorous Christian life and worship in the Roman settlements. They suggest that the Roman form of the names found in the early martyrologies and records proves nothing, for Britons had sometimes a Roman as well as a British name; and later scribes may also have given Romanized forms to British names. And they point out that the withdrawal of the Roman forces, which might have been expected on the contrary theory to have weakened or destroyed the Church in Britain by withdrawing the principal source of its strength, was in fact followed by an expansion and revival of British Christianity which preceded a very

active period of missionary work. History
affirms clearly that, from the third century
onwards, the Faith had taken firm root in
Britain ; archaeology is all but silent. The
problem awaits solution ; all that is certain
is that the record of Romano-British Christianity is not written in stone.

THE IRISH INFLUENCE

Christianity first reached Britain from
the east. But before the Church reached
any high degree of organization, and while
it was yet in the missionary stage, another
tide of influence began to set towards
Britain from the west.

How the Faith first came to Ireland we
cannot tell with any certainty. But, at a
very early date it had effected a lodgement
on those western islets which take the first
shock of the Atlantic waves. On Skellig
Michael and other crag-bound fastnesses
where it might seem impossible for man to
live, little Christian settlements arose.
Naturally, it was an austere form of Christianity which clung to those barren rocks,
on which the hermit priests and com-
munities of ascetic monks raised their
cells and oratories. There they lived in
constant struggle with those powers of
darkness in which they believed with so
simple and strong a faith ; there, too, they

found in Him Who is Light a strength
which prevailed over the powers of darkness,—

> "They had their lodges in the wilderness,
>   Or built them cells beside the shadowy sea,
>   And there they dwelt with angels."

But they were not merely solitaries, bent
on saving their souls by flight, without
regard to the world that lay beyond the
walls of their retreat. In no race has the
missionary spirit shown itself more strong
and constant than in the Irish. The early
Irish Church was one of the most active
centres of missionary activity. From their
island cells the solitaries issued, their pre-
paration at last complete, to preach the
Faith in Britain, on the Continent, even
in Iceland. From Ireland came S. Kenti-
gern to Strathclyde and North Wales,
S. Columba to Iona and the Picts, S. Fursa
to East Anglia before he passed to his
work and his death in Gaul, S. Aidan to
Iona and Lindisfarne, the source of the
conversion of the north of England. And
since we have definite traces of their
presence in places so far removed from
one another as Melrose, Burghcastle,
Malmesbury and Cornwall, it is clear
that the work of the Irish missionaries
covered a very large part of the whole
area of Britain.

They were not merely itinerant. Settling where they found it possible, in tribes of which the chiefs were friendly, they established centres of the Faith. And a centre meant a church, some sort of building for worship, however simple. The Irish traditions in building, therefore, came to have an influence on the beginnings of British architecture. The Roman influence, dating from the mission of S. Augustine, was strong ; but the Irish influence has to be taken also into account.

The first buildings of the Irish hermits and missionaries were of the rudest kind, resulting rather from the orderly heaping together of stones than from anything which can properly be termed building. So soon as the Irish began to use stone at all—and on those western islands it was often the only available material — they employed the method known as "beehive" construction, in which low round huts were reared of unmortared stone in courses that overlapped more and more until they approached the apex of the building and could be closed at the top by a slab. These buildings present the rough outline of the arch, but they show no knowledge of the construction of the true arch, and they owe their stability to the balance of the successive courses.

Their doorways had lintels supported
on uprights, or on approaching courses
of stone, again approximating, in some
instances, to the arch-form, and their
windows followed the same construction.
In this simple method of dry-stone building a great degree of skill was attained,
until, in the oratory of Gallerus, in Kerry,
we find a well-built church of walls
converging to a ridge, having ends also
converging, but in a less degree than the
side walls.

The discovery of mortar at once modified
very considerably the lines on which the
dry-built oratories and churches had been
planned. It became possible to make the
walls less thick, and to build them more
nearly upright. And, greatest advance of
all, the true arch made its appearance.
The earliest use of mortar was in all proba-
bility to fill the interstices of walls already
built of dry stone, or to fill with a core of
mortar and rubble the space between two
dry-built walls. But it was a short step
from this method of construction to that of
building proper, in which each course was
laid in mortar.

With the introduction of this new method
of building the churches began to receive
ornament, and to develop with the skill in
craftsmanship which the mason was acquir-

Plate 4.

Early Irish Work: Seven Churches, Glendalough.

ing. The builders had more confidence in
work which was evidently more stable
than the dry-built work of their predecessors, and so they were willing to expend
more labour and care upon it. A type
was evolved which continued in vogue
for a long period, and which may be illustrated by S. Columba's house at Kells, an
oblong building with a vaulted roof of
very steep external pitch, with small
windows, and with doors either square-
headed with a relieving arch in the
masonry above, or roundheaded in true
arch form, without impost between the
jambs and the arch.

Such was the Irish tradition which the
earliest missionaries brought to Britain.
Their buildings also, as on Lindisfarne,
were of the simplest kind—rough shelters
in which stone was eked out with turf
to form the walls ; or buildings of wood
merely, as the majority of churches on the
mainland of Ireland had been. The Irish
tradition, nevertheless, had an influence
on all later building in Britain in one
important point.

One of the chief differences between the
churches of the Continent and those of
England is in the plan of the east end.
In England the vast majority of our
churches are rectangular ; on the Con-

tinent it is the rule that they have an apsidal east end. For the Irish tradition was in favour of an east end rectangular ~~and~~ apsidal; and this tradition, passing to Britain with the Irish missionaries, eventually became established. The Continental tradition derived from older sources its preference for an apse. There were, indeed, exceptions; in northern France, in Swabia, and in the Rhineland the smaller churches of the Romanesque period showed sometimes a rectangular east end, but the preference was for the use of the apse. This Continental tradition of the apse reached England with the missionaries from Gaul and Italy. For a time it strove for mastery with the conflicting tradition of the square east end. But at last it was vanquished: the English builders settled down to the rectangular east end, and in the Gothic period rarely departed from it. There are other factors to be taken into account in estimating the reasons which finally decided the English custom. But the early Irish tradition must be allowed its full weight.

CHAPTER II

The First Saxon Period

THE study of Saxon work is rendered difficult by the fact that comparatively few examples remain untouched. They were sufficiently well built to endure, but they were small and rude, and since they were for the most part in places where large populations afterwards sprang up, they were either drastically altered or replaced by later and larger churches. A sufficient number remain nevertheless to illustrate the work of each period.

The earlier Christianity of Britain, which had attained some degree of organization, was swept westward by successive waves of invasion, and such scattered remnants of Christianity as survived were driven back in poverty upon mountain fastnesses. Gildas [1] suggests that there were many churches in Roman Britain, and that everywhere they were exposed to destruction. It was not until a new missionary enterprise took in hand the

[1] *De excidio Britanniæ* § 24.

18

reconversion of Britain that the art of
architecture may be said to have become
established.

S. Augustine's mission established itself
in Kent at the close of the sixth century,
and with the founding of the mission the
period which we call Saxon began. It
may be defined as lying between the
beginning of the seventh century and the
middle of the eleventh. Some buildings
which were begun before the Norman
Conquest show the effect of a strong
Norman influence, and some which were
built after the Conquest are conservative
of the Saxon character. But the Conquest
drew a clear line between the two periods,
and the exceptional cases on either side
of the line are few. For the Conquest
brought to Britain new men with new
ideas, new wealth, and the new distribution of wealth. It gave a fresh impetus to
building of all kinds, supplying the motive,
the idea, and the means. Though Saxon
and Norman work fall alike under the
general head of Romanesque, yet the conditions of the two periods were entirely
different, and the work also.

The Saxon period, then, lasted about
four centuries and a half. Certain general
characteristics survive from the earliest to
the latest work, but there were a steady

though a slow improvement in constructional methods, and divergences from the first types of plan. The evolution was not continuous. Two centuries of expansion and consolidation came to an end when, towards the end of the eighth century, the Norsemen landed in Britain and, as evidence of their spirit, sacked Lindisfarne. The invasions lasted through two centuries, first with the aim of plunder, then with that of settlement, lastly with that of complete conquest. The fury of the Northmen prevented the building of new churches and the rebuilding of those which were destroyed, and the century and a half which followed the year 800 was far less productive of churches than the two centuries at the beginning and the century at the close of the Saxon period.

THE ROMAN INFLUENCE

The churches which were built in the south of England as a result of the work of S. Augustine and his companions naturally followed in their general lines the model with which the Italian missionaries had been familiar, that of the aisled basilica. The ruined church of Reculver, near Herne Bay, had an aisled nave and an eastern apse, to which access was

gained through a screen-arcade of three
arches. The first cathedral church of
Canterbury was also of this type. But
the basilican plan had to be modified by
the circumstances of the mission. The
fewness of the converts and their poverty
necessitated the building of smaller
churches without aisles. These also
ended in apses, and had screen-arcades
of three arches. This group was represented at Canterbury by the church of
S. Pancras, of which the remains have
recently been excavated; by the first
cathedral church of Rochester, of which
the foundations exist within and without
the western end of the present nave, and
are in part outlined upon its pavement;
by the old church of Lyminge, where
foundations remain to the south of the
present church; and in Essex by the
church of S. Peter on the Wall, to the
south of the Blackwater estuary, where
Cedd, the evangelist of the East Saxons,
built an oratory about the middle of the
seventh century. To the rectangle of the
nave, which constituted the chief member
of this plan, were added in some instances
a western porch and lateral chapels on the
north and south. These lateral chapels
gave to the church a cruciform appearance, though since the lateral chapels were

Plate 5.

Saxon Doorway and Walling : Jarrow.

(See page 24.)

rather excrescences than an integral part
of the plan the churches which possessed
them cannot in strictness be termed cruciform.

In the latter part of the seventh century
another group of churches was founded
in the north of England, following upon
the missionary labours of Wilfrid, whose
policy and work were so largely determined by his affection for Rome and his
desire to bring England into touch with
the life and culture of the capital of the
West. In A.D. 675 Benedict Biscop had
been given land for the building of a
monastery at Wearmouth, and for its prior
he obtained from Wilfrid Ceolfrid, afterwards abbot. *The Life of Ceolfrid* tells us
that the church of Wearmouth was dedicated before the departure of Benedict
and Ceolfrid for Rome in A.D. 678, and
the date of the church is therefore accur-
ately determined. Their work may still
be seen in the nave and the lower stage of
the tower, which serves as a porch. The
nave was without aisles, lofty, and of a
length considerable in proportion to its
breadth; the porch was vaulted, and was
entered through doorways in each face.
But the church differed from those of the
southern or Kentish group in that it was
terminated by a square east end, and the

chancel-arch was single, not triple. Upon
Benedict Biscop's return from Rome a
second grant of land at Jarrow was made
to him by Tunbert, and there too a monastery was begun, and its church dedicated
in A.D. 684. The long and narrow chancel
at Jarrow was formerly the aisleless nave
of the church ; the tower, between the
chancel and the present nave, was probably built over the original western porch.

Westward of these monastic foundations,
and like them on or near the banks of the
Tyne, two other churches represent the
labours of Wilfrid.   At Hexham the
foundations of Wilfrid's church were
lately uncovered when the building of the
new nave was begun. The round of the
apse was found below the chancel floor
just eastward of the present screen. The
church of Hexham was an aisled basilica
after the Roman model. Below the choir
and apse, entered by steps from the new
nave, is the original crypt, corresponding
to the *confessio* of the Roman churches.
A mile or two away is the fourth church,
Corbridge, where the tower is built over
an earlier western porch, and the original
nave remains.

In all these churches the influence of
the Roman builders in Britain is evident.
At Jarrow and Monkwearmouth the

Plate 6.

Saxon Tower and Walling: Jarrow.
(See page 24.)

E

masonry presents features like those of
the Roman work, the square stones closely
resemble the masonry of the Roman Wall
and the buildings upon it. At Hexham
there is a free use of Roman material
from the great store-city of Corstopitum,
hard by, and in the western doorway of
Corbridge the voussoirs and the mouldings
of the imposts show that the arch was
removed from a Roman building and reset
in the church, while the neighbouring
walls are of stone evidently dressed by
Roman masons. The Saxon masons were
the heirs of the Roman masons not only in
regard to material, but also in regard to
methods. The Saxon masonry was in the
line of the Roman tradition, and was much
better than that of the earlier Norman
builders. The walls were thinner, and
the work avoided excessive heaviness,
since dressed stone was used throughout
the thickness of the walls. The preference for the use of large stones was also a
tradition from the Romans, whose work
would be before the eyes of the Saxon
masons who built in the neighbourhood of
the great stations on the Wall, Cilurnum
and Borcovicus, and in the town of Corstopitum south of the Wall. In other
places the Saxon masons must have been
familiar with numberless Roman works

which have perished since the seventh century.

The baluster shafts, of which many are preserved at Monkwearmouth and Jarrow, also show Roman influence. Innumerable shafts found on Roman sites in Britain show clear signs of having been turned in a lathe, and the early Saxon shafts of Benedict Biscop's churches were turned in a similar way. Their design has much in common with the general lines of the Roman work used again by Wilfrid in his church at Hexham. The Jarrow and Monkwearmouth examples are ornamented with rings of a shallow convex moulding, symmetrically disposed in groups of two or three at intervals in the shaft; between the annular groups the shaft shows a slight swelling, and in some of the shafts the whole outline swells slightly to the middle. But these early Saxon shafts lack the bases and capitals which formed an invariable part of the design of the Roman shafts, a curious difference for which it is difficult to account, since both the general lines and the mechanical methods employed were in other respects imitated. In the upper windows of the west wall of Monkwearmouth these shafts are found at the corners of the jambs, and it is probable that most of the shafts which

now remain were removed from similar
positions. They are found also in the
jambs of the doorway to the western
porch at Monkwearmouth, where on each
side two shafts are set on a high plinth
carved with surface ornament, themselves
supporting the imposts from which the
arch springs.

At Ripon there are scantier remains of
another church of this northern group.
For at Ripon Wilfrid founded a stone
church of no little dignity, following the
Italian type. The crypt is the only part
of Wilfrid's church that now remains ;
but Dr. Browne, late Bishop of Bristol,
has little doubt that a stone now in a buttress on the north side of the present
church was the capital in one of those
porches which Eddi mentions as being
among its notable features, and it shows a
pattern which is found at Brescia in north
Italy. Like the original church of Canterbury, Ripon seems to have had its altar at
the west, after the custom followed in the
larger of the Roman churches.

Between the Kentish and the northern
groups there are two churches which demand attention. Escomb, county Durham,
has a nave long and lofty in proportion to
its width, with a narrower and square
chancel. Here too there is much use of

Plate 7.

Saxon Arches turned in Roman Tiles: Brixworth.

(See page 30.)

stone from Roman work, probably from
Vinovium, the modern Binchester, and
the quoins at the angles of the building
are of large dimensions. The chancel
arch is high, and is made of carefully-cut
voussoirs, running through the whole
thickness of the arch. The imposts are
chamfered, and the jambs of the archway
are composed of stones set alternately
upright and lengthwise. The doorways
are not arched, but have flat lintels. Their
jambs are slightly inclined as they ascend
to the lintel, a feature which is very
noticeable in the early Irish work, as in
the older of the Seven Churches at Glendalough, co. Wicklow. Lintel and jambs
are mortised into one another, in the
fashion of the Roman masons. Two of
the windows have round heads, not arched,
but cut from single stones, again in a
fashion which was followed in Ireland.
Two other windows have flat heads, and
all the windows have internal splays and
inclined jambs.

The original church of Brixworth, which
was much modified in the second Saxon
period, was at one time thought to be a
Roman basilica appropriated to the service of the Church. But though there is
much use of Roman material, it was evidently set, not by Roman masons, but by

Saxons little accustomed to its use. The arches are turned in Roman tiles awkwardly stilted where they rest on the imposts, and not set in the lines of the radii of the arch. The first church had aisles, connecting with the nave by arches. These aisles have disappeared, and in their filling windows of a later date have been inserted. Above this original arcade there is the rare feature of a clerestory, with large windows. The east end terminated in an apse, and the presbytery was entered through a triple screen-arcade, like those of the Kentish type. The remains of an ambulatory, now outside the church but formerly enclosed, seem to indicate that there was an intention to make a *confessio*, which was abandoned.

The larger of these early Saxon churches were very notable buildings. The chroniclers of the eighth century speak with admiration of their beauty, their well-polished stones, their exquisite masonry. The walls of Wilfrid's church at Hexham were full of passages and winding stairs, leading to oratories ; the floor was paved with finely-jointed stone slabs. Their high-pitched roofs were probably covered with lead, as we know that of Lindisfarne to have been. Benedict Biscop sent to Gaul for workers in glass, at that time unknown

in England, for the glazing of the windows
of his churches and monasteries; he himself brought from the Continent many
books, vessels, and pictures of great beauty
for its furnishing. In religion and in religious art this early period was a golden
age of the English Church.

SAXON FONTS

The number of indisputably Saxon fonts
remaining to-day in English churches is
very small. The earliest missionaries of
Britain baptized in streams and lakes;
and when churches were built and fonts
placed in them as a necessary part of their
furniture these fonts were probably simple
wooden tubs. Mr. Francis Bond, in his
exhaustive work on fonts, produces evidence from documents, carvings, and
tapestries to show that in France tubs of
hooped staves were used for baptism,
and their use was probably general over
Western Europe. Not only are early fonts
of stone very often of tub-shape, preserv-
ing in another material the lines of their
predecessors, but in continental marble
fonts dating from the eleventh century
the staves and hoops of a wooden tub are
imitated.

These wooden fonts perhaps lasted in
many churches until a comparatively late

period, when they were replaced by fonts
of a late Norman or Gothic type. Some
early fonts of stone must have perished
with the destruction of the churches in
the Danish invasions. Others again were
rejected for aesthetic reasons, the old
fonts being set aside or broken up to
make room for better. Yet Mr. Bond's
researches have led him to the conclusion
that the number of pre-Conquest fonts is
larger than hitherto has been supposed, and
it is possible that a few fonts which have
been attributed to early Norman workers
are in reality of Saxon origin.

One about which no uncertainty can be
felt is to be seen in the remote and most
interesting mountain church of Partrishow
in Breconshire. It bears a Latin inscription to record that Menhir made it in the
time of Cynhyllyn, and the font dates
from the time of the consecration of the
church in the middle of the eleventh century, before the Norman influence had
reached Breconshire. The font has departed from the tub-form, and is rudely
shaped with base, shaft, and bowl. The
inscription is cut round the rim.

Characteristic ornament on a few other
fonts enables them to be assigned with
some degree of certainty to the Saxon
period, though allowance must be made

F

for the survival of ornament and methods
of craftsmanship in isolated districts after
they had been abandoned elsewhere. The
Deerhurst font, with its pattern of Celtic
spirals, is most probably pre-Conquest,
and is at least a fine example of its type.
Bingley in Yorkshire has what is probably
a font, though its use has been questioned,
showing an interlacing pattern of early
type. So clumsy a font as that of Mor-
wenstow can scarcely have been the work
of Norman masons; and other fonts, as
that at Curdworth, exhibit ornament of a
rude, archaic, and probably pre-Conquest
design.

THE SECOND SAXON PERIOD

By the end of the seventh century
the Church in England had passed
from the missionary to the settled stage.
But with the death of Theodore in
A.D. 690 and of Wilfrid in A.D. 709
a period of extraordinary energy came
to an end. The Church in the eighth
century could scarcely do more than
keep what in the seventh century she
had won. Great names adorned her
annals, as those of Bede, Egbert, and
Alcuin, yet at the end of the eighth
century she was growing cold, perhaps
as the result of her comparative isola-

Plate 8.

Early Font : Partrishow, Breconshire.
(See page 33.)

tion from the larger life of the West, zeal among regular and secular clergy alike was decaying, and with it the fervour of the layfolk.   The Danish invaders found England an easy prey, and in a century of persecution churches and monasteries were blotted out, scarce any of importance were built.   Not until the victories of Alfred did the land begin to hope again.   Then a revival of religion followed the establishment of peace, and the influence of. Dunstan directed the new energy of the Church.

The saints of the troubled times, as S. Swithun, are credited with the building of many churches, but importance cannot be attached to lives written long after by enthusiastic biographers.   Very few churches can be certainly dated within this long period.   Towards its close the church of S. Michael at St. Albans may have a date about A.D. 950 assigned to it, for the name of the abbot who built it is known.   But it was not until the reign of Edgar, who ascended the throne in A.D. 957, that a fresh era of church building began.   Edgar was no less zealous than his friend and counsellor Dunstan in the work of reform and restoration, and the life of the Church was renewed.

Even before the Danish invasions the direct influence of Italy and Gaul upon England had begun to decline. In the early part of the eighth century scholars from Germany came to the school of York, made famous by Archbishop Ethelbert and Archbishop Egbert. An earlier Egbert had sent Willibrord on a mission to the Frisians; Boniface left England to begin his great work in central and southern Germany. Boniface kept in close touch with England, and consecrated Englishmen to the bishoprics which he founded. Willihad, a Northumbrian missionary, had been supported by Charlemagne, and died Bishop of Bremen. Missions sent to Germany in such force involved a constant intercourse between the two countries.

From Austrasia, the eastern division of the Frankish Empire, England received a new artistic impulse. Charlemagne had there fostered the arts; and the Austrasian school drew its earlier inspiration from Rome, Ravenna, and the East, to be reinforced later by the energy of the Lombard masons.

It was, then, from German rather than from French or Italian sources that many of those features which we regard as characteristic of Saxon work were derived.

England drew from Austrasia inspiration
and practical help.   To take but one
instance — Benedict Biscop had, in the
seventh century, sent for glass-workers
from Gaul ; his successor in the next
century, Abbot Cuthbert, obtained glass-
workers through his countryman Lul, at
Mainz on the Rhine.

Among the few churches that can be
affirmed with some certainty to belong
to the Danish period is the ruined
chapel of Heysham on Morecambe Bay,
which represents the Irish influence,
and is indeed dedicated in honour of S.
Patrick.   It was a long rectangular building, with no division between nave and
chancel ; it shows the corbel at the base
of the gable which is common in early
Irish work, and was intended to carry
the projecting eave of the wooden roof.
Among other churches which Professor
Brown places within this period are Ave-
bury in Wiltshire, Bishopstone in Sussex,
where there is a large lateral porch, and
S. Mildred's at Canterbury, where large
stones are used for the quoins.   But
the dates of all these are still open to
question.

With the revival of building in the tenth
century the distinctive features of the
later Saxon work, including those which

Plate 9.

Base of Tower and West Doorway: Earl's Barton.

(See page 41.)

were derived from Austrasia, made their
appearance. Western towers were built
upon the porches of earlier churches, as at
Monkwearmouth and Corbridge. In new
churches the western tower becomes an
important member of the plan, as in a
Lincolnshire group of churches. In
another important group the tower is not
a subsidiary member of the plan, but is
itself the body of the original church.
This was probably the case at Barnack.
At Barton-on-Humber the tower, which
has received later additions, was the body
of the church, with a chancel smaller in
area projecting on the eastern side, and
a western projection of about the same
area as the chancel, supplementing the
tower space, and entered through the
tower, in which was the principal door.
But this type of centralized plan, which
has its parallels in Germany, was only
applicable to small churches. English
skill in building had not yet developed to
the point when a central space could be
made sufficient to accommodate more than
a few worshippers, and after a few experiments the centralized plan was
abandoned.

Another type of tower is that to which
the term axial is applied. The base of an
axial tower forms a division of the church,

and its walls are on the exterior flush with
the walls of the nave or chancel, though
on the interior they show the thickening
necessary to support the weight of the
upper stages. The churches of Diddle-
bury, Shropshire, and Hooton Pagnell,
Yorkshire, have their axial towers at the
west end. At Dunham Magna, Norfolk,
there is an axial tower between the nave
and chancel. Weybourn, Norfolk, has an
axial tower of which the lowest stage
formed the chancel.

Other variants from the plain rectangular plan appear as the age advances.
The western porch tends to lose its importance with the development of the
lateral porch towards the western end of
the south side. It is true that many of the
existing Saxon churches have a principal
doorway in the west face of the tower, as
at Earl's Barton, but others show a south
porch of some dignity, and this arrangement prevailed, as being most suited to
a land where west winds are frequent.
Lateral chapels, whether or not serving
also the purpose of entrance porches,
suggested the cruciform plan in which
these chapels are not merely excrescences,
but communicate by wide arches with
a central space, though the idea of the
transeptal church with central tower was

G

not fully grasped and widely applied until after the Conquest.

Development of plan can only be studied when there is opportunity of comparing the plans of many churches. There are, however, in the later Saxon work salient differences from the earlier which at once arrest the attention. It is in these differ-ences in the detail of construction and ornament that the Austrasian influence becomes clear.

The earlier masonry of large squared stones was very generally abandoned for the use of rubble masonry with thick joints. This was, nevertheless, so well constructed that it was still possible to keep the walls comparatively thin.

The use of large stones for the quoins was superseded by the use of long-and-short work. Rectangular slabs of stone, bonding well into the masonry of the wall, were set alternately with long upright stones, square in section. This arrange-ment is now very clearly seen in the angles of the tower at Earl's Barton. But a close examination of this work shows that the horizontal slabs project slightly at the angles, exactly corresponding with the upright stones where they touch, but slightly cut back as they leave the angle and are bonded in the walling. The faces of the wall were originally plastered to the line of the face of the uprights, so that the stones which now show as horizontal and vertical were then seen as long and short, the greater part of the horizontal slabs being concealed by the plaster.

The towers of Earl's Barton and Barnack exhibit another characteristic feature of this period, in the pilaster strips with which the faces of the tower are covered. These strips are ornamental merely, and not constructive buttressing. It was thought by earlier writers on Saxon work that they might have been derived from the wooden construction in which the Scandinavians were expert, but this theory has been disproved. It is more probable that they were derived from the Austrasian "lisenen," which, in their turn, were descended from the small pilasters supporting straight-sided arches, which occur in late classical buildings of the Carolingian age. In the Saxon work they have lost the classical bases and capitals of their predecessors, and show only blocks of squared stone at their bases and heads, nor are their faces ornamented with fluting. But the derivation is at least probable. At Earl's Barton these pilaster strips project from the present surface of the wall, but when the original plaster, of which we have already spoken as concealing the construction of the long-and-short work, was in place the pilaster strips must have shown as very shallow ornament, either barely projecting from, or actually flush with, the wall surface.

The upper windows of Earl's Barton tower show a third characteristic feature. They are of five lights, each of which has a round head cut from a single stone. These are supported on baluster shafts advanced to the line of the wall, swelling between the three rings with which they are ornamented. The shafts do not carry the whole weight of the wall above, which is supported at the back of the window opening by plainer and concealed shafts. Similar baluster shafts, without the concealed shafts, are seen in the interior opening of the tower to the nave at Brixworth, in the late Saxon alterations of the original church. Other forms of window-opening are seen in the towers of Barnack and Earl's Barton, with triangular, round, and segmental heads.

The walls, as at Earl's Barton, rise from insignificant plinths, having but one or two courses of slight projection. The upper edges of these plinth courses were sometimes chamfered, as at Wareham and Stow, sometimes left square,

Plate 10.

Saxon Tower : Earl's Barton.
(See page 43.)

as at Earl's Barton. The artistic value
of an emphasized base to a heavy building had not yet been discerned. The
principal doorways show some degree
of elaboration. At Earl's Barton the
pilaster strips which run up the sides
of the doorway are continued arch-
wise over the head, and within this
there is a roll moulding springing from
squared imposts. The jambs are of large
flat stones, at right angles to the wall.
Doorways of triangular heads, formed by
the inclination of two stones, are found
at Holy Trinity, Colchester, and other
churches.

Scarcely any Saxon towers show clearly
how they were originally capped, for most
have been altered or raised in subsequent
centuries. But at Sompting, in Sussex, the
original arrangement is clear, though the
spire was shortened in the eighteenth
century. Here the tower walls run up
into gables, and from each gable starts
a ridge of a pyramidal spire, of which the
flat sides descend to the angles of the
tower, at the start of the gables. In the
middle of the faces of the tower are
pilasters, ascending to the apex of each
gable, and the survival of similar pilasters
in the truncated tower of S. Benet's, Cambridge, seems to Professor Brown to

prove that this tower was finished like
Sompting, with a German helm. Other
towers may have had simpler pyramidal
caps starting from level walls, or saddle-
backed roofs, based on two gables and two
flat-topped walls. But little can definitely
be said on the point.

To this period belong several noteworthy churches besides those which
have been mentioned. Deerhurst Priory,
near Tewkesbury, had an early western
tower, lateral chapels, and an eastern apse.
The windows from the tower to the nave
have triangular heads, and show surface
ornament distinctly classical in character.
Bradford-on-Avon has a rectangular nave
and chancel, with lateral porch-chapels
of large size, in which the entrance doorway is pierced westward of the middle of
the porch, in order to give space for an
altar against the east wall. The walls of
the church are divided horizontally by
a string-course, below which there are
pilaster-strips, and above which is shallow
arcading, not constructional, but cut as
ornament upon the walls as soon as they
were completed. The jambs of the doorways are slightly inclined, the church is
lofty in proportion to the width of the
building, the chancel arch is narrow and
rests upon square imposts. Worth, in

Plate 11.

Saxon Tower with Helm : Sompting.
(See page 46.)

Sussex, is the unique instance of a complete Saxon church, with lateral chapels entered only from the church, and an eastern apse. It is unaltered, for the later tower does not trench upon the original plan. The chancel is unusually wide, its voussoirs run the whole depth of the arch, and both the chancel arch and those which give access to the chapels have square imposts of exceptionally massive character.

THE THIRD SAXON PERIOD

The Saxon work undertaken after the peace of Wedmore in A.D. 879 had brought some measure of quietness to the land is less interesting than that which preceded it. At the beginning of the period the threads of tradition were being painfully picked up, at its close France was again exerting a strong influence upon English art. Canute's pilgrimage to Rome had set the example for many Englishmen, clerical and lay, and the relations between the Continent and England became closer. The accession of Edward the Confessor involved the increase of Norman influence. Himself brought up in Normandy, he was Norman in every sympathy. He set Normans in high places, both in Church and realm,

H

and with them began that Norman influence upon English building which gradually increased until the Conquest made it
dominant.

At the close of the tenth century Saxon
work had already lost many of its earlier
characteristics. The apse had been
practically abandoned in favour of the
rectangular end. It occurs at Deerhurst,
where there was originally an apse to the
chancel, and an apse also to the south
chapel, but _rarely elsewhere. Aisles
were no longer built, the normal church
plan was that of an aisleless nave and a
rectangular chancel, entered by an arch of
greater width than had formerly been
customary. The screen arcade of the
basilican and Kentish plans had left no
successor, and crypts were no longer a
feature of the more important churches.

Against these losses may be set the
growth in importance and dignity of the
western tower. Its ground stage served
as a porch for the western entrance. Its
upper stages seem often to have been used
as living rooms, as at Brixworth, where
the tower was heightened after the Danish
troubles. These towers were tall and
narrow. Their outline was not softened
by buttresses, the absence of a strong
base-course gave them an appearance of

Plate 12.

West End, with Window Openings from Tower : Brixworth.
(See page 50.)

instability. They were divided into stages
by rude string-courses, above which the
tower was slightly set in, so as to give
the tower a tapering effect. The sole
ornament is found in the doorways and
window openings, which are small and
few. The window openings are cut
straight through the wall, and show
usually two round-headed openings, between which the wall above is supported
by a flat through-stone, running from the
exterior to the interior wall-face. This
through-stone is supported by a mid-wall
shaft, cylindrical, square, octagonal, or
baluster in form, with caps of the square
form, rounded underneath, which was
afterwards so common in Norman work,
and which is known as the cushion cap.
What ornament the cap receives is of
rude volutes, scallops, and simple reeding.
The smaller windows are often double-
splayed from a point midway in the
thickness of the wall, though the single
splay to the inner surface of the wall is
also found.

There is in Lincolnshire an interesting
group of late Saxon towers, of which the
towers of S. Mary-le-Wigford and S.
Peter-at-Gowts, Lincoln, are the best
known. These Lincolnshire towers are
lofty and slender, unbuttressed, with

double window openings and mid-wall
shafts. Pilaster work has all but disappeared from the group, the quoining
is of oblong stones, instead of long-and-
short work. The windows are splayed
internally, the tooling of the stone suggests
Norman rather than Saxon methods,
and herring-bone work—an indication of
Norman influence—is found. The whole
group is indubitably Saxon, but in its
departure from the normal type of Saxon
work Mr. Hamilton Thompson sees clear
evidence of the spread of Norman influence among English masons before the
Conquest.

That influence must, in any event, have
increased with the general recognition of
the superiority of the Norman work to
the Saxon. And there were at last
political and ecclesiastical influences which
fostered it. Edward the Confessor began
in 1050 the West minster, which as the
Anglo-Saxon Chronicle records, was consecrated a few days before his death.
"About mid-winter (i.e. of 1065) King
Edward came to Westminster, and had
the minster there consecrated, which he
had himself built to the honour of God,
and S. Peter, and all God's saints. This
church-hallowing was on Childermass
day." For its building Normans were

employed, and the fashion of so great and central a church would have been widely followed. But the conquest of England in the following year involved the complete supersession of the rude Saxon type of Romanesque—a backward member of the family, as Mr. Bond has termed it—by the more advanced Norman.

CHAPTER III

The Coming of the Normans

THE Conquest brought England at once into the full current of Western European thought and life. Ecclesiastics regular and secular swarmed into England, took possession of the Church as William had of the realm, and emulated one another in the setting-out and building of large churches. The parcelling-out of the possessions of the conquered placed enormous resources at the disposal of the builders; nor, indeed, had the Orders and the prelates been poor when they left Normandy. Never before or since has there been such an outburst of activity in building. The population of England numbered then less than three millions, yet the land was soon set thickly with churches, many of which were of vast size. Even to-day, when many of the Norman churches have disappeared, there are wide tracts of England where one is never out of sight of a church containing at least traces of Norman work; and when we consider that the rude methods of that age neces-

sitated the employment of far more men
in quarrying, dressing, transporting, and
setting stone, we might almost imagine
that the entire population of the country
had given itself to the work.

In the fifty years which followed the
Conquest there were built, or rebuilt, of
the great Benedictine churches, Canterbury, St. Albans, Rochester, Winchester,
Ely, Gloucester, Malvern, Tewkesbury,
Worcester, Pershore, Bury St. Edmunds,
Chester, Durham, Norwich, Sherborne,
Peterborough, and Romsey; of churches
served by canons secular or regular, Hereford, Lincoln, York, S. Paul's, S. Davids,
Chichester, Christ Church, Hants, Southwell, Carlisle, Bangor, Waltham, Exeter,
and Llandaff. All are churches of the first
rank. No great pre-Conquest church was
left untouched in the Norman period, with
the exception of Hexham. And in the
case of many of these vast churches the
scale on which they were first set out was
sufficient for the needs and the ambition
of the Middle Ages. The Normans were
not content to build churches which might
afterwards be extended if the need arose;
their first designs were on the grand scale.
In later centuries the great churches were
extended eastward, for practical and ceremonial reasons; presbyteries were length-

ened and Lady chapels were enlarged, but nothing was added to the length of the naves of Canterbury and Lincoln. Sometimes, indeed—as at Bath—the later rebuilders were content with a smaller area. The Norman Romanesque builders set the standard of size for the Gothic.

Yet the long list of great churches represents but a part of the activity. Wherever manors were granted to knights there churches were built or rebuilt, served often by Norman priests who displaced the English with as little compunction as the Norman prelates felt when they were intruded into English sees. It seemed to them to be the merest duty to possess the land. The Conquest had been presented to them as a religious war, waged against a perjured usurper; the Pope had blessed it; William had posed as a champion of the Church; ecclesiastics had furnished him with ships and men. They were but entering upon their own, and at least such men as Lanfranc and Anselm made the Church in England radiant with new glories.

THE PLAN OF THE LARGER NORMAN CHURCHES

With the Conquest came a strong wave of Benedictine influence. The Archbishops

I

Lanfranc and Anselm were Benedictines, the Conqueror placed the larger monasteries under zealous Norman abbots, the cathedral priories were reconstituted. The planning of the great minsters, therefore, followed closely the lines which had been settled in Normandy; and it was in them that the foreign influence was most directly felt. Their planning was conformed to types worked out and accepted on the Continent. The long nave, limited only in width by the possibilities of obtaining long timbers for the tie-beams, was flanked by aisles. In the eastern arm of the church the apse reappeared, to begin again that struggle for naturalization in England in which it had been defeated before and would be defeated again. For a century after the Conquest the exceptions to the Norman rule that great churches should end in an apse are fewer than half a dozen. The choir, like the nave, was flanked by aisles. But in the planning of the eastern arm of the church two distinct methods of treating the main apse in conjunction with the choir aisles were employed.

The first is that known as the parallel apse plan. It seems to have been derived originally from the East, and to have passed to Lombardy in the ninth century, and thence down the Rhine and to France.

Plate 13.

West Front : Ely Cathedral.
(See page 62.)

In this plan the choir aisles terminated
each in its own apse, extending no further
eastward than the chord of the main apse.
Upon this plan were set out the eastern
arms of Canterbury, St. Albans, Durham,
and Peterborough, to mention typical
examples. But of this parallel-apse plan
no example remains unaltered. At Peterborough the main apse exists, but the
apses of the aisles were superseded by
rectangular chapels towards the close of
the thirteenth century, and the east walls
of these were removed when the extension
known as " The New Building " was made
in the fifteenth century.

The second method of setting out the
eastern arm is known as the periapsidal
plan. In this arrangement the choir aisles
do not end in chapels, but are carried
round the apse, forming an ambulatory
or procession path. From this ambulatory
project chapels, usually three in number,
their axial lines running north-east, east,
and south-east. Of this type the cathedral churches of Gloucester and Norwich
present good examples. At Gloucester
the lateral radiating chapels remain, the
eastern chapel has been superseded by
larger and later Lady chapels. But in the
crypt the arrangement can be seen unaltered, for when the Lady chapel was built

the crypt was not extended. At Norwich, also, the main apse, procession path, and lateral radiating chapels remain; but the original eastern chapel gave place to a larger in the thirteenth century, itself to be removed about 1570.

The periapsidal plan presented practical advantages over the parallel apse plan. It was the need of more chapels and of a procession path which necessitated the rearrangement in later centuries of many churches which had at first been planned with parallel apses. It was suited to monastic churches, and was used for the church at Leominster, where its foundations remain eastward of the present chancel end.

From these two types of planning for the greater churches there was practically no deviation in the early decades of the Norman period. Romsey is sometimes accounted an exception. But it is probable that the early cruciform apsidal church, of which traces remain beneath the tower, was the first Norman church, and that the present rectangular east end and ambulatory are a rebuilding of about 1120.

The transepts of the larger churches were conceived on the same generous scale. They had aisles on the east, from

each of which projected usually a single
chapel, as at Gloucester and Norwich,
or less frequently two chapels, as at
St. Albans, where the arches through
which the chapels were entered remain,
though the chapels disappeared before
the sixteenth century. In this type of
transeptal plan the chapels nearest the
choir were slightly longer than those
beyond them. S. Mary's, York, like St.
Albans, had two transeptal chapels on
each side, arranged *en échelon* to group
with the eastern apse and aisle chapels.
The eastern aisles at Durham, Ely,
Peterborough and Norman Lincoln, were
divided into chapels and had no projecting apses. At Ely and Winchester the
chapels have western aisles also, and
the arcades of the aisles are continued
round the transept ends to support a kind
of gallery, a feature borrowed from such
Norman churches as the Abbaye aux
Hommes at Caen. At Ely there was
also a western transept, of which the
southern arm remains. This western
transept, which served as model for
Gothic plans, gave abutment to a western
tower, and presented a west front of no
little dignity. It had also two apsidal
chapels, parallel with the nave aisles.
These Mr. Bond considers to have been

ritualistically objectionable, because so remote. Yet they were no further from the sacristy than the chapels at the extreme east, and their vestments were probably kept in chests near the altar.

In the large cruciform churches a central tower of square and heavy type was raised above the transept crossing. A great proportion of these central towers fell, some soon after their erection, as that of Winchester; others in the later Middle Ages, as that of Ely, where the happy accident of the fall of the Norman tower gave Alan of Walsingham the opportunity of designing the lantern which is the glory not of Ely only, but of England. Various causes contributed to their ruin. The distribution of weights upon piers and thrusts through buttresses had not yet been scientifically worked out, faulty foundations were often responsible for rapid settlements, and Norman masonry was often far from excellent. It is characteristic of Rivoira's theorizing that he attributes the fall of Winchester tower to the fact that English masons were not sufficiently capable craftsmen to carry out the splendid design of the Norman master masons.

The central tower, if it be properly designed, is a valuable element in the

construction of a cruciform church. Its
mass serves to counteract the pressure
exerted towards the centre of the church
by the various arcades, while the arcades
in turn give some abutment to the tower,
and there results that playing off of thrust
against thrust upon which the whole
science of Gothic architecture depends.
So, too, the western towers at the ends
of the aisles serve to counteract the thrust
of the nave arcades, as at Southwell.
Exeter and the later imitation of Exeter
at Ottery St. Mary present a striking
deviation from the normal rule of the
central tower, for there the lower stages
of flanking towers are themselves the
transepts.

THE PLAN OF THE SMALLER CHURCHES

In the planning of the smaller and parochial churches the Normans exercised a
less direct influence. No general rebuilding of the parish churches began immediately after the Conquest, as had been
the case with the minsters. The Norman
priests were the chaplains of the knights,
their altars were in the chapels of the
castles and manor houses. The parochial
system was not definitely settled until the
twelfth century; and it was in that century
that the wave of architectural activity

K

reached the parishes into which the
country had then been parcelled out. By
that time several types of parish church
were fully developed, of which some
were in the line of the English tradition,
and others had been accepted in Normandy.

The English tradition still produced
churches with rectangular chancels, western towers, and aisleless naves. In these
churches the extension of the Norman
influence is seen in the increased width
and lessened length of the nave, which
in earlier ages had been long and narrow.
The south doorway, with its sheltering
porch, superseded the western entrance
under the tower, and the Norman west
tower was often built without any doorway into the church, or with one reserved
for ceremonial use. The earlier Norman
chancels remained short, but there are
now very few early Norman rectangular
chancels which received no addition to
their length in the thirteenth or fourteenth
centuries, as at Aymestrey, Herefordshire,
and Avening, Gloucestershire, the latter a
good example of a vaulted Norman chancel
which has been lengthened by a bay in
the thirteenth century. By the middle of
the twelfth century, however, Norman
chancels were being built which proved

quite adequate to the developed ceremonial of later times.

The chancel arch is generally an important feature in a Norman church. But
there are some examples of oblong
churches with no structural division between nave and chancel, as the church
of S. Peter, Northampton.

With the English tradition of the rectangular chancel the Norman preference
for the apse contended in vain, in the
parish churches. The apsed Norman
churches are distributed fairly evenly
over England ; but in no region are there
many, and by the end of the period the
apse was practically disused in England.
The Norman builders arrived in England
already expert in planning and building
apses; the English builders never cared
for the apsidal plan sufficiently to master
the difficulties which it presented.

In some of the smaller Norman churches
there reappears the threefold division of
the church into nave, choir, and chancel
which existed in the earlier Saxon work.
Of this Iffley presents a familiar example.
Here there is a tower over the choir, and
both the arches which the plan necessitates are elaborately ornamented. More
often the threefold division of the church
is found in conjunction with an apse, as at

Kilpeck, than with a square end as at Iffley.

In the plan of the smaller parochial churches is seen the passive strength of the insular tradition and the proof that the work was done by local masons. For the plan which would most have commended itself to the Norman builder makes but a rare appearance in rural England, and the aisled cruciform church, with a tower at the crossing, is represented by few examples. The constructional difficulties would, perhaps, have determined the adhesion to the traditional plan. But there must also have been a realization of the fact that the aisled cruciform plan is not very suitable to parochial worship. In a large cruciform church—cathedral or monastic—the whole church was broken up into divisions, and the eastern arm with the high altar constituted in effect a church reserved for the monks or canons; while the layfolk could hear Mass at the many minor altars westward of the choir. But in a cruciform parish church the high altar was parochial, the altar of the Mass at which there was the largest congregation; and there was a distinct disadvantage in interposing between the high altar and the bulk of the people the massive piers and low arches

Plate 15.

Chancel Arch and Apse : Kilpeck.
(See pages 67-8.)

of the transept crossing. The insular
type, then, prevailed in parochial churches
as well by reason of its practical advantages as by the simplicity of its constructional problems.

NORMAN PAROCHIAL CHAPELS

One result of the rapid development of
the organization of the Church in the century which followed the coming of the
Normans was the provision of a large
number of parochial chapels within the
vast areas of the Saxon parishes. Sometimes these chapels were in close proximity
to the manor-house of a great landowner;
in other cases they were built in order
that the Church might reach with her
ministrations those who lived far from the
parish churches. Their fabrics conform
with great regularity to one type, though
they differ in size, and still more in the
degree of their ornament. The type is
that of a rectangular building with square-
ended chancel, without any "priest's
door," a fairly wide and plain chancel-
arch, and an aisleless nave rather wider
than the chancel, and about twice as long
as its breadth. There is but one doorway
in the building, and that is on the south
side; the windows are small and widely

Plate 16.

The Heath Chapel: Shropshire.

(See page 73.)

splayed, and they were originally provided with shutters in lieu of glass.

These chapels were subordinated with some strictness to the parish churches, upon whose rights of burial they were restrained from encroaching. There were, therefore, no graveyards attached to them, at any rate on their foundation, and marriages were solemnized only in the mother church of the parish, and not in the chapels. The chapels had fonts, lest any child should die unbaptized, and on ordinary days Mass was said in them, but on the great festivals all parishioners were under obligation to resort to the mother church. In the course of time some of these chapels became parochially independent, usually at an early stage in their history; their priests were advanced to the status of perpetual curates or vicars, and as the population around them increased the chapels were enlarged or rebuilt. Others, again, fell into ruin and disappeared, or their walls became incorporated in farmhouses or barns, as was the case with the chapel of Dode in Kent.

But here and there an example still exists of a Norman parochial chapel unaltered and in use. One such may be found in the parish of Stoke St. Milborough, between Ludlow and Much

Wenlock in Shropshire. The Chapel of
the Heath was built in the days of William
Rufus, probably by a Fitz John, Lord
of the Manor, at the very end of the
eleventh century. It preserves its original
status of a chapelry; its fabric has come
down to us almost unaltered, for no population grew up around it. It is of the type
described, a complete early Norman building of a simple character. The nave
measures twenty-nine feet by sixteen, the
chancel seventeen feet by thirteen. It has
a good south doorway recessed in two
orders, with shafts in each jamb; the arch
above is enriched with a chevron moulding enclosing a plain tympanum. The
chancel arch is five feet three inches
across, it is carried on two shafts on each
side with slightly-carved caps, the arch
itself being quite plain. All the original
windows are of one type, narrow round-
headed openings with a wide internal
splay. Two small openings high up in the
west gable must have lighted a chamber
above the flat ceiling which once covered
the nave. The walls are relieved extern-
ally by flat pilaster buttresses, those in the
middle of the end walls being pierced by
the tiny east and west windows. The font
is certainly as old as the church, and is of
a very simple type. The Heath Chapel

L

is the type of many similar parochial chapels which have been remodelled or have altogether disappeared.

NORMAN ROOFS AND VAULTS

Some of the earliest stone buildings in these islands, as we have seen, had roofs of stone, independent of the principle of the arch, and too rude in construction to be properly termed vaults. They left no successors. The ideas which they might have suggested were not seized and worked out, roofs of wood with no vault below them became the normal covering of Saxon churches.

On the Continent the earlier Romanesque builders were everywhere confronted with the work of the Romans, who had employed domes and vaults of various kinds. Increasing mastery in the art of building enabled them to imitate the older vaulting, and they would at once see that vaulting gave to a church not only a more dignified interior, but also a protection against a constant danger. Until modern times the risks of fire were very great. The towns were built largely of timbered houses, thatched roofs were common, and in the absence of adequate means of dealing with outbreaks of a fire a whole town might easily be

involved. Even the larger and loftier
buildings would not be completely pro-
tected by their greater height. The use
of lead for the outermost covering of the
roof necessitated the frequent attention of
the plumber, with his clumsy brazier and
incurable carelessness. There were no
lightning conductors to safeguard towers
and gables, and the churches were often
struck by lightning and fired. When a
building with a wooden roof is destroyed
by fire the tops of the walls are seriously
injured, and the fall of the roof leaves a
burning mass on the floor of the church to
calcine the bases of walls and pillars. But
the roof may be burned above a vaulted
building without doing anything like the
same amount of damage.

The case of Chichester cathedral offers
an example of mishap and its useful lessons.
There was a consecration there in 1184,
after extensive building. Two years later
the roof and the wooden ceiling were set
on fire. The clerestory was damaged for
the whole length of the church on its inner
side, the blazing roof broke the string-
courses in its fall, and calcined the arcades.
The clerestory had to be refaced, and also
the piers, arches, and spandrels of the
arcade; and to prevent a similar catas-
trophe in the future the whole of the

church was vaulted when the repairs after the fire were taken in hand.

The Norman builders had, therefore, a strong incentive to vault their churches, and ancient models which they might follow. Roman vaulting was everywhere before their eyes. Before the Norman Romanesque had approached the height of its power France had already many churches which were vaulted in a series of domes or in a continuous barrel vault. The abbey which S. Edward built at Westminster had vaulted aisles, and possibly a high vault over the nave, therein differing from Jumiéges, upon which it was modelled. But the high nave vault presented difficulties from which the builders of the Romanesque churches in England usually shrank. At Ely and Peterborough they were content to vault the aisles, and to ceil the nave with a flat ceiling under a wooden roof. At Durham, as we shall see, they were more bold.

Two types of vaulting had reached some degree of development on the Continent before the Conquest. The barrel vault is the simpler. It is merely a prolonged semicircular arch, tunnel-shaped, and supported throughout its length on two parallel walls. Upon these walls the vault exercises an even outward thrust for the whole

of their length. It requires, therefore, very
strong walls for its support, and it would
be rash to weaken them by piercing them
for windows of large size. Nor would
external buttressing strengthen them
scientifically, since the pressure of the
vault is continuous, and not concentrated
upon points where buttresses could meet
the additional strain. The barrel vault,
then, has very obvious disadvantages, and
though it was adopted for a number of
French churches its use in England was
limited. The Chapel of S. John in the
Tower presents an example ; the aisles in
the nave of Fountains are vaulted with
pointed barrel vaults running at right
angles to the axis of the church. But its
use was chiefly in covering passages and
small buildings, those especially which
had abutment from buildings on either
side.

The groined vault was free from many
of the disadvantages of the barrel vault.
It presents the appearance of two barrel
vaults intersecting at right angles, the
curved lines produced by their intersection
being the groins. In this type of vault
there is no such continuous pressure upon
the walls as the barrel vault exercises, the
weight. of the vault is collected at the
corners, and since the vault is practically

a homogeneous mass of masonry there is comparatively little thrust. If, therefore, the weight were adequately carried at the four corners, the intermediate spaces of the wall could be considerably reduced in thickness, and it became safe to insert doorways and windows more in number and of larger size. The groined vault had been employed by the Romans, who had become expert and daring in its construction. But their skill had been lost, and the Romanesque builders had to start afresh and proceed tentatively to achieve the same end. And before they had attained to the mastery which the Romans had shown, the science of vaulting had so developed that the groined vault was abandoned ; though in buildings which were some time in hand the use of the groined vault was continued until the end, as in the nave aisles of Ely.

The Ely work is indeed an excellent example of groined vaulting. Transverse arches of stone run from the great piers to the aisle walls, dividing the aisles into square bays. The groined vault fills each space bounded east and west by the transverse arches, north and south by the nave arcade and the aisle wall, where there are longitudinal arches. The transverse arches are not essential to the construction

Plate 17.

Late Norman Vaulting: Christ Church, Oxford.
(See page 82.)

and stability of groined vaulting; but they
strengthen it, and they have, as will be
seen in the aisles of Ely, an artistic value,
breaking the smooth surfaces which a
groined vault presents, and giving effects
of light and shade. Practice soon made
the Normans perfect in the art of vaulting
comparatively small spaces, and they were
able to cover not only square and oblong
spaces, but irregular and curved spaces
also, as in the ambulatory at Norwich.

The groined vault was more scientific
and more beautiful than the barrel vault,
but it had limitations of a narrow kind.
Its construction necessitated the use of
very cumbrous centering. To build a
groined vault it was necessary to construct
first an exact model or mould in wood.
Upon this centering, raised with difficulty
to its place upon the springers of the pro-
posed vault, the rubble of the vaulting was
set, and only when the whole was complete was the vault secure. The centering
was then removed, and set up again for
the next bay. In England wood was
plentiful enough. The English builders
were not compelled, as the Romans had
been in places, and as the builders of
Lombardy afterwards, to devise methods
which should economize their scanty store
of wood. But even in England the labour

of shaping large centerings of wood with
the rude tools of the time, and of continually setting up and taking down the massive centering, was sufficient to stimulate
the minds of the builders to invent some
method of erecting a vault which should
dispense with the necessity of centering
for the whole area of it. There are also
constructional weaknesses in a groined
vault of which they must have been well
aware. It is imperfectly arcuated, the
solid mass is borne on four points, but it
needs support rather than abutment. Its
diagonal lines, being longer than the semicircular arches which bound the bay, are
not true semicircles, but elliptical, or de-
pressed curves. The lines of the groined
vault die out at its crown in a flattish space
which suggests a weakness actually present, and even to the early builders its
effect was so unsatisfactory that in some
vaults, as in the older bays of the crypt
at Rochester, the lines of the groining
are pinched down, so as to give them
prominence and an appearance of greater
strength.

It might seem but a short and unimportant step from the groined vault to the
vault in which the lines of the groin are
replaced by stone ribs. Those who took
that step were doubtless glad to find a

M

simple way out of an old difficulty. But
the change involved a revolution in constructional methods. The first builders of
ribbed vaults in England were altering the
whole course of architectural history, and
making possible the supreme achievements
of the later Gothic.

With the introduction of the rib, groined
vaulting ceased to be used, except for
buildings already partly covered with it,
as the aisles of Ely. It had never been
used in England for wide spaces, and its
limitations had been understood. Before
taking leave of it we may observe that
the term is often misapplied to include
vaults of all kinds. Groined vaulting is
that vaulting only which is without ribs.
The systems of the rib and the groin
are in reality absolutely different, for in
groined vaulting the interpenetration of
the vaulting surfaces determined the lines
of the groins, but in rib-vaulting the ribs
determine the shapes and curves of the
vaulting surfaces.

It is uncertain where the rib-vault, used
in immature forms by the Roman builders,
was revived. Lombardy is the probable
place of origin, but Porter says that it was
never used there with enthusiasm, and
that there is not a single Lombard church
extant in which it is used throughout.

Yet at San Nazzaro, Sesia, the nave of the
church was rib-vaulted in 1040, and Rivoira
gives San Flaviano, Montefiascone, five or
six years earlier in date, as the earliest
church with rib-vaults of which the date
is certain. But in the eleventh century
builders in many places were at work
upon the solution of a problem which per-
plexed them all ; nor, in spite of Rivoira's
opinion, is there any reason why the problem should not have been solved indepen-
dently at Durham. That problem was the
elimination of the massive centering which
made groined vault laborious to erect.

In a bay of rib-vaulting the centering is
needed only for the diagonal arches of
stone which are first built. When these
diagonal arches or ribs are finished, the
web, or filling-in, of the vault can be set
upon them. The four triangular divisions
into which the arched ribs divide the bay
can be dealt with in turn, one by one, and
the only centering needed for the web is a
small, expanding instrument called a cerce,
formed of curved pieces of wood, slotted
and clamped, each with an angle-iron at
its end, which can be hung on the stone
ribs to form the centering for each course
of the web, and then moved on, slightly
contracted, to form the centering for
another course. Each course of the web

is itself slightly arched from rib to rib, so
that the web keeps its place.

Vaults of great strength can be built
upon ribs in this way. It was a method
of skeleton construction, in which the ribs
were the essential part, as may be seen in
many a ruined church where the ribs
remain from which the web has fallen
away. But the web was itself constructed
with great care, so solidly indeed that in
other ruins we may see large portions of
vaulting from which the ribs have been
torn away. The rib-vault is very elastic,
and allows for a considerable amount of
distortion when settlements take place in
its supports and abutments. If it should
be so endangered as to need extensive
repair, each compartment can be dealt
with separately. It responds to every
demand of design, and can be adapted
easily to the most irregular spaces, as the
intricate and delightful vaulting of the
retrochoir at Wells proved in later centuries.

Durham is the home of the rib-vault in
England. The history of the Durham
vaults has been worked out by Mr. Bilson
in a paper which has become one of the
classics of the history of vaulting. There
the choir-aisles had been rib-vaulted so
early as 1096, and the high vault of the

Plate 18.

Early Norman North Transept: Winchester Cathedral.
(See page 90.)

choir by 1104. By 1133 the whole of the
building had been covered with rib-
vaulting of wide span and with pointed
arches, the first great church in Europe.
Here some master-mind was evidently at
work. Bishop William of St. Carileph,
exiled to Normandy for his share in the
rising against William Rufus, cannot have
brought back the idea from Normandy,
for there were no ribbed vaults there
much earlier than the middle of the twelfth
century. But it is possible, as Rivoira
suggests, that he visited Montefiascone
when he went to Rome as envoy of the
Conqueror, and brought the idea from
San Flaviano. However that may be, the
credit of working out the idea indepen-
dently at Durham belongs to his master
mason. There was a certain hesitation in
planning them, the high vaults were not
decided upon until the walls were far
advanced, but once enterprised they were
carried through with courage and skill.

For their vaults the Durham builders
definitely adopted the pointed arch, compelled to do so by the exigences of their
work. The use of the pointed arch enables
a space to be vaulted throughout by arches
which start from their imposts and finish
at the ridge; fidelity to the semicircular
arch necessitates the stilting of some upon

their imposts, and the depressing of others
to weak segmental curves, as may be seen
in the choir aisles of Peterborough. The
transverse arches of the nave at Durham
are pointed; those of the transepts are
stilted semicircles, as, almost certainly,
were those of the original high vault of
the choir. The omission of the intermediate transverse arches is due to the
alternation of the circular columns with
the main shafted piers throughout the
church; the difficulty which this causes
in the setting-out of the vault is seen in
the aisles of the choir.

The example which the daring builders
of Durham had set waited long for followers. Their high vaults had few successors elsewhere in Norman times, but
there was a high vault at Lincoln in 1140,
and in some great churches, as Peterborough, shafts and other preparations
were made for high vaults which were
never built. The glories of Durham are
unrivalled and unimitated, and even
Rivoira, constantly depreciative of the
English work, pays them a meed of
qualified praise.

NORMAN WALLS AND BUTTRESSES

The Norman masonry was inferior to
the Saxon, for it was not of dressed stone

throughout. The core of the wall was constructed of rubble, the faces of ashlar, following a method inherited from the Romans. A wall so built may be strong or weak. Much depends upon the bonding of the faces with the core, much also upon the quality of the mortar which is used for the rubble. Some Norman mortar remains to-day as hard as the stone which it binds ; other Norman mortar has gone to dust, pouring out from the interior of the wall or pier when the face is cracked or removed. This method of construction necessitated thick walls, and the Norman walls therefore are more massive than those of their predecessors, though their appearance of relatively greater strength is misleading. The stones used for the faces of the wall are commonly of small size, since they were often transported from distant quarries by water, or on packhorse or cart over the roughest of tracks. An improvement in methods of transport may be indicated by the use of larger stones in the latter work. The stone was dressed not with chisel or saw, but with picks, the final surface being given with an axe furnished with teeth on its edge, and used diagonally across the face of the stone. In the work which immediately followed the Conquest the

Plate 19.

Apse and Corbel-table : Kilpeck.
(See page 92.)

joints of the masonry were thick.   But
in this, as in the bonding of the faces
with the core, the later Norman work
showed a considerable improvement. The
more even dressing of the stone enabled
the mason to work with less mortar and
thinner joints, and the whole work became
more solid. The new type of thin-jointed
masonry seemed wonderful to those who
saw it for the first time; William of
Malmesbury speaks of the masonry of
Malmesbury so carefully and exactly set
that you might think the whole building
to be of one stone. The difference between the old and the new may be clearly
seen in the north transept of Winchester.
There the masonry of the northern bay is
of Walkelin's building.   The fall of the
tower in 1107 tore away parts of the
transepts, and in the rebuilt portions the
narrow-jointed work contrasts with the
wide-jointed work of the uninjured bay.
That much of the Norman masonry was
very good is proved by the fact that the
Gothic builders piled heavy superstruc-
tures upon it, far in excess of the weights
which it was designed to carry: that
much also was very bad was proved long
ago by its fall from inability to bear even
its own weight.

But the failures were due sometimes to

defective foundations rather than to the quality of the masonry. The Norman practice in regard to foundations was as variable as the masonry. Peterborough, though it stood without underpinning until our own time, has foundations of the most shallow kind, though a few feet below the surface there was solid rock. At Hereford and Lincoln, on the other hand, are examples of Norman minsters upon admirable foundations, scientifically planned and carefully constructed.

The ground courses of the walls and towers were as yet unemphasized. Neither Saxon nor Norman realized that the weight of their walls required distribution upon broad bases, both for stability and for artistic effect. It was not until late in the period, when a fresh stream of influence flowed in from Burgundy, that they began to show a more generous projection. String-courses were much used, partly to protect the walls from the unchecked flow of rain down them, partly also because they gave relief to the flatness of walls unbroken by large buttresses and windows. The square profile of the string-course which the Saxons had used was softened in the later Romanesque by chamfering its upper and lower edges, by hollowing the lower surface, or by giving to the whole string-course a roll form.

It was usual to advance the upper courses of the wall upon a corbel table, to give support to the projecting eaves of the roof, by which alone the rainwater was thrown clear of the walls. Both in the larger and the smaller churches these corbel tables are of great interest and variety. At Iffley the corbels are simple blocks, at Barfreston and Kilpeck they are treated with individual carving of masks and grotesques; at S. Sepulchre's, Cambridge, and Southwell Minster the corbel table assumes a continuous wavy form; at Ely the west front shows a form of arched corbel table which was very generally used.

The buttress becomes of importance only when the Romanesque is in transition to Gothic. It was not absolutely essential until the development of rib-vaulting necessitated the transmission to the ground of the thrusts of the vaults collected at definite points in the wall. The walls of the earlier Romanesque builders were expected to furnish both support and abutment by their continuous mass. The early Norman buttress had but a slight projection from the wall. Even groined vaults did not develop the

Plate 20.

The Round : S. Sepulchre's, Cambridge.

buttress, for they called for vertical support rather than lateral abutment, and we
see that in the aisle walls of the Ely nave
the buttresses are no more prominent than
they would have been if there had been
no vault.

As with vaulting, so with buttressing,
the Romanesque builders had to redis-
cover for themselves what the Romans
had known, and their immediate successors had forgotten. The pilaster strip
which the Saxons had taken over from
Austrasian sources was of hardly less constructive value than its derivative, the
small buttress which the Normans used.
Not till after the middle of the twelfth
century did the buttress begin the logical
development which ended in such work as
King's College Chapel, Cambridge, where
the buttresses appear as spur walls, while
the wall between them has almost disappeared with the growth of the window.
Yet the early Norman builders may
have dimly discerned the coming importance of the buttress. They set shafts at
its angles by way of decoration, and their
principles were sufficiently sound to prevent the emphasis by decoration of features which were wholly unimportant.
More than the shafts they could not
attempt, for the buttress was as yet

untapered, it had no stages or set-offs, upon which the later types of buttress ornament depended, and its vertical lines were only broken when the string-courses of the walls were carried round it, as at the Heath Chapel and Kilpeck.

When the high vault of the choir was constructed at Durham, it was seen that the outward thrusts must be met, or the clerestory walls would give way. Semicircular arches were therefore built above the triforium of the choir. By the time that the high vault of the nave was taken in hand the builders had come to the conclusion that transverse arches were not really very effective, and that a half arch supporting a straight upper surface inclined towards the point whence the vault sprang would answer the purpose as well or better. The nave triforium therefore has these half-arches. The Durham builders had made a second discovery of enormous importance. They had invented the flying buttress, upon which the later development of the high vault in aisled churches depended.

NORMAN WALL ORNAMENT

The ornament of the wall surface was never neglected, when resources allowed it. String-courses and dripstones, though

their function is primarily utilitarian, constitute ornament, for they break up the
flat surfaces, and they were ornamented
on their faces with carving in low relief, presenting those simple patterns
which are found everywhere in the handi-
craft of undeveloped races, and with which
the elementary art of chip-carving makes
us familiar to-day. Rochester Cathedral
shows another type of ornament in the
spandrels of the triforium arcade, where
diaper patterns were applied during the
later years of the Romanesque period
to earlier work; and the west wall
had at one time similar ornament, parts of
which are now in the crypt. Arcading
was a form of ornament which the Saxons
had used, as at Bradford-on-Avon, and
which the Normans developed both for
exterior and interior wall faces. From
the single-arch arcade, seen at Lincoln, the
arcade of intersecting arches was evolved,
and it became extraordinarily popular.
Norman arcading can be very well
studied at Ely Cathedral. In the interior
there is a continuous arcading of single
arches beneath the aisle windows. In the
chapel of the south-west transept there
is a tier of simple arcading surmounted
by another tier of intersecting arcading.
The west face of the west transept shows

Plate 21.

Norman Arcade: Tewkesbury Abbey.
(See page 100.)

a variety of types—single, single arches in pairs under containing arches, and in the later work of the upper stages trefoiled and recessed arcading, while there is some diaper ornament between the lower parts of the arcade. The interiors always, and the exteriors usually, were plastered over rubble, and the plaster was painted in the interiors. The Normans, and their successors down to the middle of the nineteenth century, had not that inexplicable delight in naked rubble walls which distinguished the Victorian restorers, and caused them to hack away plaster which in some cases was that which the Normans had laid on.

BAY DESIGN OF THE LARGER NORMAN CHURCHES

The bay design of an aisled church conforms to one of two types. It may be two-storied, with a clerestory above the main arcade; or it may be three-storied, with a triforium intervening between the main arcade and the clerestory. The two-storied type is that of the overwhelming majority of parish churches, the three-storied type is that of the cathedral or abbey church of first rank.

A Norman church of large size had usually vaulted aisles with a triforium chamber occupying the space above the vault of the aisles and below the lean-to aisle roof, opening to the nave above the main arcade, with a lesser arcade of its own. There were exceptions: at Rochester, and one or two other places, the aisles are not vaulted but have wooden roofs, and there is no triforium chamber, merely a triforium arcade with a passage in the thickness of the wall, of some interest as being the earliest instance in this country of the pointed arch in actual construction. The triforium chamber, which was the common arrangement, gave a great deal of space, usually wasted, though at Gloucester there were altars in the triforium. It had other disadvantages, for it added to the cold draughts of the building. But it had a very noble effect.

The triforium can be treated in various ways. The aisle walls may be stopped above the level of the vaulting, and the lean-to roofs taken up from that point to the level of the top of the triforium arcade, as at Southwell. Or the aisle walls may be carried up higher, allowing of the insertion of windows to light the triforium chamber, and through the triforium arcade the nave itself. Or again, the triforium may have no arcade opening upon the nave, as in the Cistercian churches, which show a blank wall to the nave. Behind this blank or decorated wall the triforium chamber may be reduced to a mere passage way.

The division of the total height of the bay varied greatly in different types of Norman design. At Norwich and Ely we have a type in which the main arcade, triforium, and clerestory approximate closely in height. The nave is well lighted by the aisle windows, the triforium windows and those of the clerestory. At Gloucester and Tewkesbury the triforium stage is not lighted, and the nave arcade is carried up to a great height, in order to allow of large aisle windows. In this design the arches of the main arcade seem absurdly small in proportion to the gigantic pillars on which they are carried, and the triforium is reduced to the narrowest compass. At Durham the arcade, triforium, and clerestory diminish in height as they ascend, and this is perhaps the most satisfactory arrangement.

The triforium arcade had sometimes one arch opening to the nave in each bay, as at Southwell, where, however, there seems to have been some intention of subdividing the opening. But the usual arrangement was to subdivide the open-

Plate 22.

Norman Piers: St. Albans.
(See page 104.)

ing into two arches under one containing
arch, as at Ely, or into four arches under
two containing arches, as in the dwarfed
triforium of Gloucester. Variants of the
normal designs are found, where exceptional circumstances called for them. At
Christ Church, Oxford, it seems to have
been found impossible to carry the church
to any great height, and the triforium
arcade has therefore been constructed
under the main arcade, in order not to
dwarf the three stages of the building.
The Oxford construction is paralleled at
Glastonbury, and in some churches of the
Austin canons, as in the choir of Jedburgh.
The effect is to make what is really a
three-storied building into one which is
apparently two-storied.

THE NORMAN PIER ARCADE

In an aisled church the pier arcade is
necessarily an important feature. It must
be sufficiently strong to bear the weight of
the clerestory wall above, and its share of
the weight and thrust of the roof and
vaults; it ought not to be unduly massive,
or the interior effect of the church will be
heavy.

The form of the earlier and simpler
arcades suggests that arched openings
have been pierced in a wall rather than

Plate 23.

Norman Clerestory : Christ Church, Oxford.
(See page 102.)

that arches have been raised upon piers. In some Pembrokeshire churches, indeed, the arcades seem to have been hewn through rubble; there is no attempt at ornament, or even at fine masonry. Nothing so rude as this appears in Norman work, but in the earlier part of the period the wall is prominent, and the piers are constructionally sections of the wall, as at St. Albans. In the nave arcade at Chichester a considerable advance has been made. The small columns in the jambs and the vaulting shafts are later additions, made after the great fire of 1186; but we can see that in the original arrangement the arcade had the appearance of arches set at intervals in a length of wall rather than borne upon piers. In the nave of Peterborough the wall spaces have become smaller, the vaulting shafts and those which correspond to the orders of the arch assert themselves more boldly, and the pier has become practically a compound pier, made up of several members; but there is still a lingering suggestion of the wall surface. That soon disappears, and in the nave of Ely the compound pier of many members has become an accomplished fact.

This development is traceable even in the English work. But the compound

pier had before the Conquest reached
an advanced stage in evolution, as such
work as the abbey church of Bernay
shows.

The evolution of the compound pier
depends upon the evolution of the recessed arch, and of the vaulting which
necessitated the vaulting shaft. When
the arch is recessed in orders it is inevit-
able that the pier which carries it shall
be brought into correspondence with it,
or there will be wasted masonry and
unsightly spaces. In Saxon times there
had been some empirical attempts at the
recessing of the arch; the Normans
brought with them the knowledge of its
value and of its construction. The recessed arch, like many another artistic
gain in architecture, was the outcome of
a search for simplicity in construction.
As in vaulting, so in arch construction,
the aim of the builder was to dispense,
as far as possible, with wooden centering.
An arch such as the Saxons had been
accustomed to use, having stones running
from one face of the arch to the other,
necessitated a wooden centering of equal
width with the arch. But the Normans
discovered that a recessed arch needed
only a narrow centering for the inner-
most order, upon which, as upon a stone

P

permanent centering, the other orders
of the arch might be successively built.
The discovery was in every way of
great importance. Arches deeply recessed
give pleasant effects of light and shade,
breaking up what would otherwise be
plain surfaces, and softening harsh out-
lines. When each of the orders of
the arch is brought down upon its
own part of the abacus, and its lines
are continued in the pier below, the
arcade has reached a point from which
all the developments, which are usually
simplifications, of the Gothic arcade
logically proceed.

But during the evolution of the compound pier in the Norman work in England there was employed also the cylindrical pier, a remote derivative of the
classical column which had been used,
or re-used, as spoil from older buildings,
in the churches of Italy. The cylindrical
pier was employed in England before the
end of the eleventh century, before its use
had become at all general in Normandy;
and Rivoira gives the nave of Malvern
Priory Church as the earliest employment
of it in England in a church of large size.
The Malvern type is short and thick, the
Gloucester and Tewkesbury type is elon-
gated, since there the arcades had to be

Plate 24.

Norman Arcade : Malvern Priory.

(See page 106.)

heightened. At Durham the cylindrical
pier alternates with the compound pier,
in that division of the principal bays
which is the peculiarity of Durham ; but
the fashion did not find followers, except
in a few of the larger churches.   The
cylindrical piers at Durham are remark-
able for their ornament of spiral lines,
both double and single, and reeding.
This, too, was a fashion which did not
become popular in England ; and there is
perhaps more beauty in the plain surface
of a cylindrical pier, giving pleasant and
soft lights and shadows, and serving as
a foil to the ornament of capital and arch,
than in the ornament which the Durham
workers applied to it. Less frequently
the cylindrical pier is found alternating
with the octagonal, as in the choir of
Peterborough.

BASES

Neither aesthetic nor practical considera-
tions determined the form of the earlier
Norman bases. As their walls and towers
were left without adequately proportioned
ground courses, bearing relation to the
mass and weight which they carried, so also
were the piers. There was a feeling that
the supports of the arcade should not rise
directly from the ground ; but the Nor-

mans had not fully realized the functions
of the base, which are to distribute the
weight concentrated in the piers and to
convey an impression of perfect stability.
So at Chichester the piers, treated in effect
as walling, have no bases, though the subsidiary shafts have. In most of the great
Norman arcades the bases are still rudimentary, as in the Winchester transepts,
even when the capitals have attained some
degree of development ; and in the minor
arcades, as in the arcading of the interior
of the tower at Norwich, the bases are
little more than suggested. The cylindrical pier was usually set upon a low,
squared plinth, of which the upper edge
might be chamfered; and the pier was
connected with the plinth by the simplest
possible mouldings, of one roll, or two
rolls separated by a shallow hollow, the
latter a reminiscence of the classical
"Attic base." The corners left by the
imposition of the cylindrical pier upon
the square plinth were filled with spurs
of foliage of a flat and simple kind. But
it may be said that up to the end of the
Romanesque period the aesthetic importance of the base was scarcely recognized,
and only the entry of a fresh stream of
influence from France secured for it the
importance it deserved.

Plate 25.

Late Norman Arcade : Buildwas Abbey.

CAPITALS

The capital, on the other hand, received constant care, and underwent a process of steady elaboration. The builders experimented boldly along several lines, and some types of later Romanesque capitals are very beautiful indeed.

A simple and therefore common form of early Norman capital is that known as the cubical or cushion capital. It is formed by rounding off the lower corners of a square to meet a circular shaft of less diameter than the square, the accommodation, in fact, of a square to a circle. It is simplicity itself, and on small shafts the effect is very pleasant. The flat surfaces were decorated in colour, and the decoration probably suggested development of the sculpture. It was a simple matter to divide the faces of the larger cubical capitals into two or three, to meet an equal number of shafts beneath. This division suggested the multiplication of parts, the breaking-up of the whole face into scallops, until the capital became a group of inverted cones, sometimes, as at St. Davids, incurved to the pier and hollowed into trumpet form.

In another type of capital the outline of the cushion remains, but its whole surface, from the lower edge of the abacus to the neck-mould which intervenes between the capital and the shaft, is covered with shallow interlaced ornament. Of this type S. Peter's, Northampton, shows some fine examples. It is a very beautiful form of decoration, suggesting affinity on the one hand with the Celtic interlaced work, and on the other, in regard at least to the general effect of the capital, with the work of the school of Ravenna.

A third type of capital was evidently suggested by the classical Corinthian capital, of which, in its Romanized form, examples remained wherever the empire had extended. Little volutes appear beneath the angles of the abacus, often absurdly small by comparison with the surfaces on which they appear. Gradually, and as the chisel replaced the mason's axe, the volutes are more boldly worked, made to project further from the face of the capital, and more deeply undercut.

The Normans had a strong preference for the rectangular abacus, using it even when it could only be adapted clumsily to a large cylindrical pier, where it recalls the Puritan objection to a square cap on a round head. In the case of recessed arches it was soon seen that a square abacus left a good deal of unused space,

Norman Capitals : S. Peter's, Northampton.
(See page 112.)

Q

bearing no weight ; and the abacus had
its angles cut back to correspond with the
orders of the arch.   But, even in such
early work as the nave of Malvern Priory
Church, logic prevailed ; and the abacus
of a circular pier was itself made circular.
Experiments in relieving the vertical face
of the circular abacus with grooves and
chamfers led by insensible degrees to the
moulded abacus of the Gothic period.

THE ORNAMENT OF THE ARCH

The compound arch, recessed usually in
three orders, though at Winchester in two
only, was a great advance upon the simple
arch, both artistically and from the point
of view of construction.   Moreover, it
was seen to offer further opportunities
for ornament which were soon utilized.
The soffit, or inner surface of the arch,
was a field on which ornament would be
thrown away, though a few examples at
Steyning and elsewhere may be found,
to prove local perversity.   But the faces
of the orders admitted of enrichment,
and it was applied to them in great variety,
and with more ingenuity than restraint.
The discontinuous enrichment employed
by the Normans was not well adapted to
the arch, of which the beauty consists in
flowing lines and sweeping curves which

ought not to be obscured or interrupted. In particular, the chevron or zigzag moulding which the Normans used so profusely and unthinkingly ruins the effect of an arch when it is seen in profile, giving a serrated and fussy effect. The most fitting ornament of the arch is a continuous moulding, as the later Romanesque builders perceived. The chamfering of the sharp edges of the orders was an obvious way of ornamenting the arch. Even here necessity may have been the mother of invention, and the chamfer may owe its origin, as Mr. Bond surmises, to the accidental chipping of the squared edges, and the desire of the masons to remedy the damage by removing the edge altogether.

For the simple chamfer, which, however, lasted on throughout the Gothic period, commended by its simplicity and cheapness, a roll moulding was substituted, and its use became very common. The Saxons had made some use of it. The introduction of ribbed vaulting doubtless suggested the use of similar moulding in the arches of the arcade; the semicircular members of the compound pier may also have suggested like forms in the arches above. At first worked singly on the edge of the voussoirs, these rolls were soon multiplied, though the Romanesque builders never attained any skill in the combination of rolls of varying size, alternating with hollows. The development of complex arch-moulding belongs to the next age.

NORMAN WINDOWS

Certain characteristics of window-openings are common to the Saxon and Norman Romanesque. After the Conquest the double window opening with mid-wall shaft was still retained for a time in towers, though with the difference that the Normans recessed the arches of the heads so that they could be brought down to the shaft without the very long through-stone, which presented obvious points of weakness. The mid-wall shaft was not, of course, suitable for windows in the body of the church, which had to be shuttered or glazed, and these were of the round-headed form. The double splay also persisted for a time, but it was ultimately superseded by the window splayed only internally.

The external face of the window was long kept within quite small dimensions, especially in the smaller churches. Though glass was procurable it was expensive, and such substitutes as linen were unsatisfactory. When glass was used it was not always set in rebates in the stone, but was placed in wooden frames, which were subsequently wedged into the window-openings, as appears from the Ely Sacrist rolls, where windows made in this way were paid for so late as the year 1292. When it was fixed in rebates the glass was set a little back from the line of the wall-face to give it protection, and to prevent the rain which streamed down the wall from driving in at the junction of glass and stone. - The string-course was sometimes carried over the head of a Norman window, and this afforded protection, as a dripstone, but in small churches the dripstone was often omitted. Protection against forcible entry may also have determined in some degree the small size of the windows, but this can have been only a secondary consideration.

One window was normally assigned to each bay, both of aisles and clerestories. In parish churches the windows were often set eight or ten feet above the floor-level. Even when they were widely splayed very little light would reach the lower part of the church; but it must be remembered that there was then no close following of the service by the congregation with the aid of books, so that a building which would to us seem quite inadequately lighted would have perfectly contented a twelfth-century worshipper.

The east and west ends of churches, and the north and south ends of their transepts, gave opportunity for simple groupings of windows, from which in later times traceried windows were to take their rise. They are found disposed in tiers, usually of three, their wide splays meeting in the interior. Variety was gained by raising the head of the middle window, or by surmounting the group by a circular light, or less often by a vesica-shaped light, as at Ashford Carbonell near Ludlow. At Iffley the west end has the unusual arrangement of a large circular light over the doorway, and above that a range of three windows, the middle one slightly higher and much wider than those which flank it. Circular windows were generally plain, but at Barfreston and a few other places a kind of tracery is found, of bars radiating from a centre, wheelwise.

Romanesque windows in England never attained the large size of the Continental Romanesque. But they increased in size as the period advanced, and it was natural that they should share in the more general application of ornament. At Kilpeck, where the window-heads are cut from single stones of exceptional size, a simple

Plate 27.

West Front: Iffley.
(See page 118.)

rounded moulding runs round the window, having rudimentary bases but no capitals. Romsey offers examples of windows having shafts at the edges of their external faces, with bases and capitals, carrying an ornamental arch-mould round the head of the window. This type of ornament was applied also to the interior of the windows, but less frequently. Iffley shows in its west front windows well developed; they are recessed in four orders, of which the outermost is carried on shafts with spiral ornament and elaborate capitals, the three inner orders receiving zigzag enrichment. Windows often appear as openings in an arcade. The Norman builders were continually experimenting upon the exteriors of their churches, and the curious disposition of the windows in the Norman tower at Bury St. Edmunds, in relation to the arches which enclose them, and to the elevation generally, is worthy of examination.

NORMAN DOORWAYS

In primitive types of building the normal way of constructing a doorway is by placing a horizontal lintel on two upright jambs. This trabeated or beam construction is the principle of all Greek building. But it is not a method which is logically or scien-

Plate 28.

Tympanum, Western Processional Doorway: Ely Cathedral.
(See page 122.)

R

tifically applied to stone construction. A
wooden beam, possessed of elasticity by
reason of its long grain and closeness of
fibre, can bear heavy weights placed upon
it. Stone employed in long bars is liable
to fracture under weight.

The earlier builders used the lintel for
their doorways. They perceived the constructive weakness of the lintel, and
reinforced it by inclining the uprights
towards the head of the doorway, as in
the Irish work at Glendalough, so as to
reduce the length of the lintel. The
Romanesque builders employed two other
methods to relieve the lintel, separately
or in conjunction. Corbels were used to
support it at either end, and a relieving
arch was built above the head of the doorway to transmit to either side of the lintel
the weight of the wall above. In the
famous "Prior's Door" at Ely, properly
the western processional doorway, the
corbel and the relieving arch are both
seen in their developed state.

The lintel tended to disappear even
before the end of the Romanesque period.
But the tympanum fought for existence,
dying out in such forms as that at Climp-
ing and Rievaulx, where the tympana
have lost the lower straight edge of the
lintel, and have assumed a trefoil form.

The simple round-headed doorway was from the Conquest employed side by side with the lintelled doorway. Wherever the resources of the builders permitted the doorway was enriched. It was an obviously important feature of the church; wherever else ornament might be unnoticed, it was impossible to ignore the ornament of the doorway, and upon it the Normans lavished their skill. It was recessed in as many orders as possible, and in the later work the wall was even thickened to gain space for additional recessing. A fine example of this thickening of the wall is presented in the late Norman west front at St. Germans, Cornwall. The west doorway is recessed in no fewer than seven orders, and to get room for them the wall is advanced four feet from the line of the west front, the projection being roofed with stone and gabled above the doorway.

The enrichment of the Norman doorway is often free and exuberant. Ornament is carried round it, sometimes in excess, as in the west doorway at Iffley. Chevron and beakhead ornament is used, each member of the ornament being cut to fill a separate stone of the jamb or voussoir of the arch; and since there was no nicety in bringing the stones to one size, there is a noticeable irregularity in the run of the enrichment. Stars, pellets, cable-moulding—a derivation from Roman sources—billets, nailhead, and other varieties of enrichment are found. Kilpeck doorway presents an example of interlaced snake ornament in which the sculptor may be thought to have exceeded the limits of a reasonable freedom, since he has obscured the constructional lines of the doorway, though the effect is very rich. It must be admitted that the more elaborate examples of Norman doorways sometimes defeat their end, and that the simpler recessed doorways, with shafts at the jambs and recessed orders not overlaid with ornament, are more effective than the ambitious types in which the sculptor has obtruded his skill at the expense of the constructive lines.

Norman windows were often removed in later times to make way for larger, Norman doorways have survived in greater number. Their size and the beauty of their design satisfied other centuries than that in which they were built; and when a church was enlarged in the Middle Ages the old Romanesque doorway was often preserved, and set up in the new wall of the enlargement.

Plate 29.

Late development of the Tympanum: Rievaulx Abbey.
(See page 122.)

THE NORMAN TYMPANA

In doorways of the Norman period the shafts of the jambs often carry a lintel, and the semicircular space, or lunette, between the lintel and the enclosing arch is filled with masonry, leaving the actual doorway square-headed. The space between the lintel and the arch is known as the tympanum.

The Norman masons were quick to see that the lintel and the tympanum offered an excellent opportunity for ornament, and the treatment of the tympana constitutes an interesting field of study. The remaining examples have been carefully examined, described, and illustrated by Mr. C. E. Keyser in his authoritative work on *Norman Tympana and Lintels*, and to his book the reader may be referred for a detailed study of their ornament. It must suffice here briefly to indicate some main characteristics.

The distribution of the Norman tympana is curiously irregular. In the counties of the eastern side of England, even in those which offer many good examples of Norman work, Norman tympana are rare. But in the counties of the middle west, Gloucestershire, Worcestershire, and Herefordshire, they are very numerous, and a fair number remain in Yorkshire,

Plate 30.

Norman Doorway : Kilpeck.

(See page 124.)

Derbyshire, and Cornwall. Doubtless in those counties which have now but few remaining examples there were formerly tympana which have disappeared in rebuilding during the Middle Ages; others are known to have been destroyed even within living memory in so-called "restoration." But there must always have been a far greater proportion in the Norman work of the west and south of England than in similar work in the eastern counties. Of those that remain the larger number are in their original position, but some have been moved to other positions in the exterior walls of their churches, or have been placed within to guard them against further destruction by weather, and a few have found their way into museums.

In some instances both lintel and tympanum are plain. In others the lintel is ornamented with carving, while the tympanum is of uncarved masonry. It is probable that where this is the case the plain tympanum was at one time adorned with colour, and traces of colour remain on some of the carved tympana. The interiors of churches in the Middle Ages exhibited the use of colour and gilding on a scale which we can scarcely realize, accustomed as we are to plain masonry, the churches glowed from floor to roof with bright colour which was not restricted to flat surfaces alone, but was applied also to moulding and carving, and colour was certainly employed in some cases upon exteriors also.

In those tympana which exhibit carving the range of subjects is not wide, but there is great variety in the treatment. Some tympana are rude and simple, others show considerable mastery of design and skill in craftsmanship. A few bear inscriptions which date the work in which they occur. Among these the tympanum at Castor, recording the dedication of the church in 1124, is noteworthy.

Where there is no inscription a common subject is the cross, incised or in relief, and it is often included within a circle. A subject which is found in nearly thirty examples is the Tree of Life and Knowledge, which figures on the tympanum of the beautiful doorway at Kilpeck. It is a subject which receives the most varied treatment; sometimes the tree is realistic, sometimes so conventionalized that its significance is not at first glance apparent. In many examples the tree is flanked by animals which feed upon it, or birds are shown sheltering among its branches. Other tympana represent the animals

s

without the tree, sometimes engaged in conflict, dragons, winged serpents, lions, and monsters of quite indeterminate species.

Our Lord is represented in majesty on a number of examples, though He appears more often in symbol, as the *Agnus Dei*. The western processional doorway, known as the Prior's Door, at Ely Cathedral shows our Lord in majesty, attended by angels, and the same subject appears on the tympanum of the great west door at Rochester Cathedral, perhaps the best known of all the tympana. The Blessed Virgin and the Holy Child are found, as in a tympanum of singular dignity and artistic merit at Fownhope in Hereford-shire. Among the rarer subjects are S. Michael overcoming evil, and S. George and the Dragon, represented with great spirit at Brinsop. Apostles and evangelists also figure, and there is a small class of purely secular subjects, as hunting scenes. Old Testament subjects are rare; but at Stretton Sugwas there is one which probably represents David slaying the lion; and an almost obliterated tympanum in the old chapter house at Rochester represented the sacrifice of Isaac, as is proved by the fragment of the inscription, *aries per cornua.*

NORMAN FONTS

No period later than the Norman shows so wide a range in the design and ornament of fonts. From the rude masses of stone, cubical or cylindrical, with their upper surfaces hollowed into bowls, their sides roughly dressed and relieved by the simplest ornament or by none, to those which show masses of elaborate sculpture, the gradation is complete. For the purposes of classification they may be divided into unmounted fonts, and those which are mounted upon stems, with or without subsidiary shafts.

The unmounted fonts are usually cylindrical. In the plainer examples one or more bands of roll or cable moulding encircle the font, and constitute its sole ornament. In the more elaborate examples the whole surface may be covered with geometrical or interlacing ornament, often recalling the Celtic types, cut either in low or in high relief. Arcading makes its appearance as the period advances, sometimes extending from the base to the top of the font, in other cases surmounted by a broad band of bold and free ornament, in which the foliage motive is occasionally interspersed with faces, dragons, and mythical beasts. In later examples the arcading is often double and

Plate 31.

Norman Font: Brecon.
(See page 134.)

intersecting. The arcading suggested an opportunity for figure sculpture, and many fonts show figures of considerable boldness and skill in modelling, as that at Orleton, Herefordshire.

Cubical fonts are less common. They exhibit the same type of ornament as the cylindrical, sometimes, as at Lenton, worked out with much delicacy of execution. These unmounted fonts, both cubical and cylindrical, seem to have been set on plain plinths with the upper edge chamfered, but so many early fonts have been moved or reset that the original arrangement is often lost.

A simple form of the mounted font is that in which the bowl is set on a base resembling an inverted bowl, with a band of moulding at the narrowest part. The chalice-shape, with a bowl of which the sides are most frequently vertical, and with a stem thick in proportion to the bowl, makes an early appearance. The arcading and other ornament found on the unmounted fonts is common to these also. Another type is that in which the bowl is hollowed from a rectangular block of stone supported either upon a single thick stem or upon a thinner stem reinforced by smaller shafts at the angles of the bowl. Of this type fine examples are

found at Toftrees, Shernborne, and other
places in north-west Norfolk. In Cornwall, where font construction all through
the Middle Ages pursued a very independent line, the corner shafts are sometimes
found to run outside the angles of the
bowl, which is rounded below to meet the
central shaft, as at Roche and Bodmin,
and in this type the corner shafts have the
appearance of steadying the bowl rather
than of actually supporting it. Such fonts
as that at Brecon, in which the outline is
clear and the ornament shallow, present
a great contrast to fonts like those of
Castle Frome and Eardisley, where the
outline of the font is subordinated to the
bold and intricate ornament with which it
is covered from lip to plinth. Scriptural
subjects and figures of saints are in these
fonts varied with symbolical figures, upon
which much ingenuity of interpretation
has been expended. Doubtless many of
the strange beasts and mysterious figures
on Norman fonts symbolize the escape
of the soul of man from evil through
baptism. Thus, on fonts at Youlgreave
and Haddenham the poisonous salamander, reputed to love fire and hate
water, represents the devil driven from
the soul of the newly baptized by the
water of regeneration. The dragons

Font of Black Tournai Marble : Winchester Cathedral.
(See page 136.)

which crawl humble and abased beneath
the font at Castle Frome, and the lions
which seem crushed beneath the font at
Hereford, may have a like signification.
The men who seem to extricate themselves from entangling tendrils, the warriors who overcome monsters, may be
referred to the same general idea; and
the theme of "man's first disobedience"
and the expulsion from Paradise are subjects frequently met with on Norman
fonts, as on Norman tympana.

THE BLACK FONTS FROM TOURNAI

At Tournai on the Scheldt there was in
the latter part of the twelfth century a
workshop in which were made fonts of
a bluish-black marble quarried in the
neighbourhood. These fonts conform to
a well-marked type, closely resembling
one another both in dimensions and ornament.   They are found not only in the
Low Countries, but in Northern France,
and seven examples are to be seen in
England.   Four are in Hampshire, at
Winchester   Cathedral,   S.   Michael's,
Southampton, East Meon, and St. Mary
Bourne; two are in Lincolnshire, at the
Minster and at Thornton Curtis; one is
in Suffolk, at S. Peter's, Ipswich.   It will
be noticed that all these churches could

be reached by water-carriage, and that the fonts could therefore have been readily transported from Tournai, heavy though they were.

These fonts have square bowls, varying only from three feet three inches to three feet seven inches in diameter, and from one foot five inches to one foot seven inches in depth. The bowl is supported on a cylindrical shaft, with four smaller shafts at the corners of the bowl. The hardness of the marble has enabled them to resist damage, and they are all in good preservation, though the East Meon bowl has been reset on a fifteenth century base.

The upper surface of the bowl, between the circular bason and the angles of the square, is usually filled with a floriated ornament. The sides of the bowl are carved with a rude vigour. The fine example at Winchester Cathedral presents on two sides the legend of S. Nicholas; on the other sides are doves, grapes, and a salamander, within medallions. The East Meon font has on two sides the creation of Adam and Eve, and on the other sides an arcading, with a frieze of fishes, birds, and beasts above. The Bourne font also has arcading on two sides, with grapes on the others. The

Southampton example has three symbols
of the evangelists on one face, and on the
others mythical beasts, all in medallions.
Those at Lincoln, Thornton Curtis, and
Ipswich have a continuous ornament in
the fashion of a frieze, of lions, winged
griffins, and strange monsters. Their
ornament may be studied in detail in Mr.
Cecil H. Eden's *Black Tournai Fonts in
England.*

THE PASSING OF THE ROMANESQUE

For sixty years after the Conquest the
preponderating influence in planning and
building had been that of the Benedictines.
In 1128 the Cistercians settled at Waver-
ley, and in the next twenty years had
established a great number of houses.
They came from Burgundy; the necessity
laid upon Cistercian abbots to attend the
general chapter held annually at Citeaux
kept them in touch with the progress of
architecture in Burgundy, while their
constitutions imposed certain very definite
conditions upon the designers of their
churches. The Cistercians at once brought
a strong influence to bear upon English
architecture, especially where they were
grouped in vigorous houses like those of
Yorkshire. In their work may be found

those signs of change in construction and ornament which marked the passing of the long-lived and still vigorous Romanesque into the Gothic. The rejection of the round arch (still kept for minor arches) in favour of the pointed arch for the pier arcade, as at Fountains, Kirkstall, and Buildwas; the appearance of the keel-moulding at Roche and Byland, and of the fern-leaf capital at Abbey Dore; the bettering of the system of roof-drainage; the disposition of windows in groups which closely resemble the simpler forms of tracery, as at Kirkstall and Fountains —in all these respects the Cistercians showed themselves the inaugurators of a new manner.

In the south-east, where the Cistercians settled less closely, other forces were at work. In the Ile de France, the royal domain lying around Paris, there was a vigorous school of architecture which made its ideas felt in the choir of Canterbury, the typically French work of William of Sens, and in its derivative, the retrochoir of Chichester.

In the west the Benedictine house of Worcester was the source of a native stream of new influence, unfed by French tributaries, which by the year 1175 had decisively rejected the round arch in the pier-arcade, and had developed an essentially Gothic vault.

From these three schools came the heralds of revolt. By the last quarter of the twelfth century the power of the Romanesque in England was broken. The transition to Gothic was in full process, and would soon be accomplished. The Romanesque in England had for a long time remained tentative, immature, somewhat timid. At the last it had accomplished very noble work. In the consistent dignity of Ely nave, in the splendid daring of Durham, in the repose of small and simple country churches like Kilpeck and Adel, it had shown itself capable of great, if not the greatest, achievements. Its most noticeable characteristic, the round arch, had denied to it such flexibility as the Gothic was about to show. But Romanesque was a grave and great style, and those who used its possibilities to the full, whether on a large scale or a small, built truly in the grand manner.

Printed by A. R. Mowbray & Co. Ltd., London and Oxford

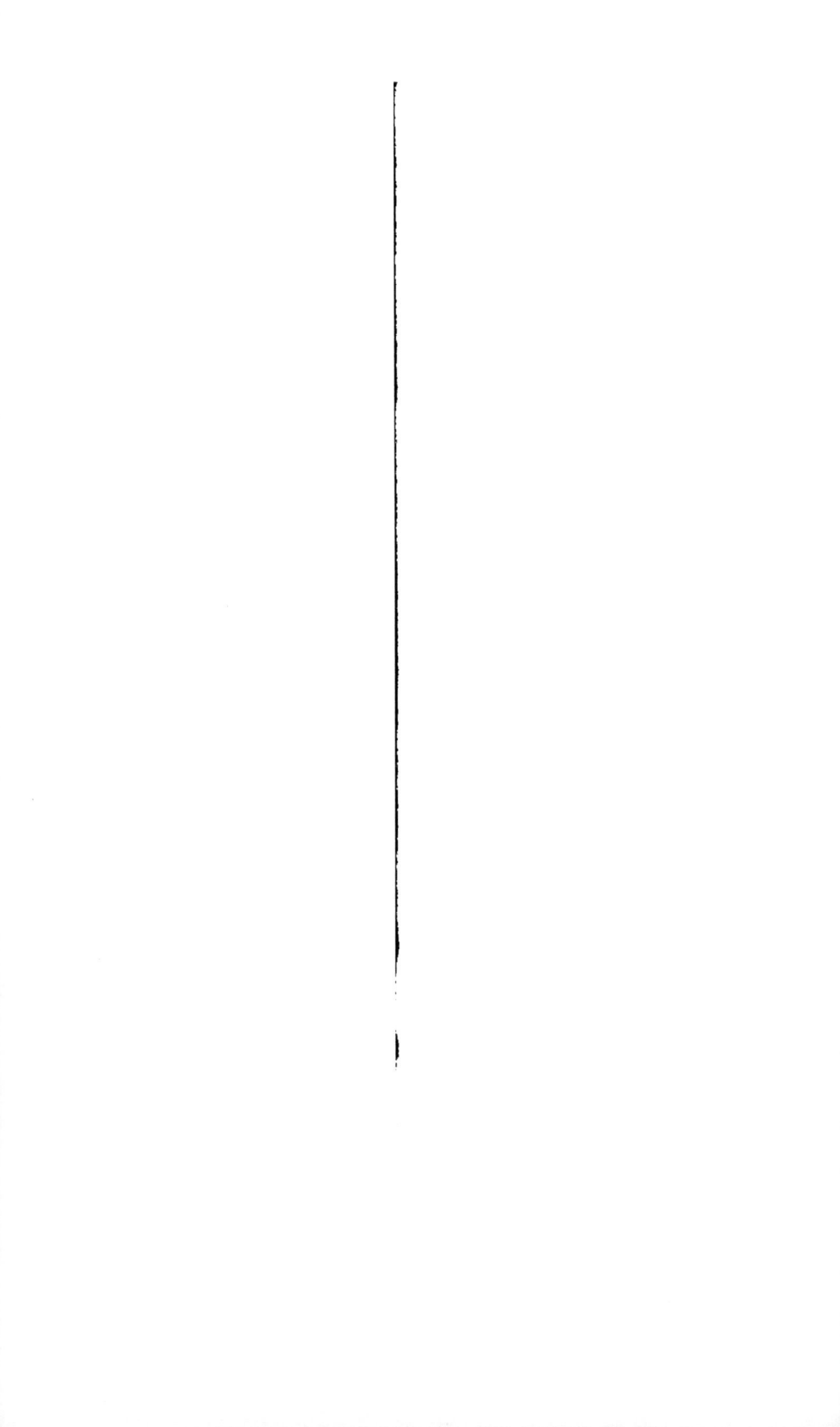